The Pocket Essential

STEVE McQUEEN

www.pocketessentials.com

First published in Great Britain 2000 by Pocket Essentials, 18 Coleswood Road, Harpenden, Herts, AL5 1EQ

Distributed in the USA by Trafalgar Square Publishing, P.O. Box 257, Howe Hill Road, North Pomfret, Vermont 05053

A CIP catalogue record for this book is available from the British Library.

ISBN 1-903047-23-4

9 8 7 6 5 4 3 2 1

Book typeset by Pdunk
Printed and bound by Cox & Wyman

for Ni, Shabby, PJ, Morro and the rest of the WGCCC IVth XI - average cricketers,
excellent friends
and for Janet & Robin - the Luck brothers' other parents

Acknowledgements

Many, many thanks to John Ashbrook for smuggling me on board and to Paul Duncan for not reporting me to the purser.

Note

Unless attributed otherwise, all quotes come from the mouth of Steve McQueen.

Contents

Screen Acting - An Essay And An Apology

"In my own mind, I'm not sure that acting is something for a grown man to be doing."

Since this book is largely about movie acting, I suppose it's only right that I should say, here and now, that I don't have a lot of screen acting experience. Indeed, I don't have much performing experience period. Besides playing a slightly confused Joseph in my infant school nativity play (my attempts to conjure up awe were stiffled by my curiosity about who the real father was) and an ebullient Major Magnus in a senior school production of Tom Stoppard's *The Real Inspector Hound* (I made Richard E Grant's Withnail look restrained), I haven't done anything that deserves to be called acting. As shoddy as my own performance record is, I'd like to think my time as a film critic (five years, man and boy) qualifies me to discuss screen acting.

There's a great myth about movie acting that, for you to be thought of as any good, you have to play extraordinary parts. Autistic East German women with limps, mentally challenged flying instructors, and gay quadriplegics, we are led to believe, are the type of parts that inspire fine acting. It's a lie that has been perpetuated by the Academy of Motion Picture Arts & Sciences dishing out best acting Oscars to a succession of turns as cripples (Daniel Day Lewis in *My Left Foot*), savants (Dustin Hoffman in *Rain Man*), foreigners (Meryl Streep - take your pick) and mutes (Holly Hunter in *The Piano* and Marlee Martin who, shock horror, actually is deaf, in *Children Of A Lesser God*). Such is Oscar's love for the healthy, American thesp playing cripples and continentals that Robin Williams (unsuccessfully nominated four times before scooping a gong for *Good Will Hunting*) once mused that: "if I keep on losing like this, I'm gonna have to play that bisexual, Spanish Olympic skier with motion sickness some time soon."

The thing is, foreign tongues and disabilities are meat and drink to actors. Sure they're very eye-catching, but any half decent performer should be able to effect a decent limp or accent (although judging from Michael Caine's performance in *The Cider House Rules*, simply speaking in an accent other than your own, no matter how ridiculous, is sufficient). It's a much, much harder task to create fully-realised, three-dimensional human beings, as indicated by the struggle Hoffman and Streep encounter when it comes to playing 'normal.'

The other big thing about screen acting is that, when it's good, you really oughtn't to realise the actors are acting. Like the very best special effects, great acting should absorb you to the point that you're unaware it's artificial. Richard Attenborough, a co-star and close friend of Steve McQueen's and no mean turn himself, once said that: "there's nothing worse than watching a performer and then thinking; 'well, that was very impressive.' The moment you find yourself admiring a performance, you know the actor's failed to do his job properly."

The only thing worse than a performer who draws attention to him or herself, is an actor who can't act. Given that movies are a multi-billion dollar business, it's amazing just how many inadequate performers there are making decent livings in Hollywood. While shite performances abound in the City Of Angels, it's important to make a distinction between people who can't act and people who 'play themselves.' James Coburn, Burt Reynolds, Terence Stamp, John Wayne and Oliver Reed are just five of the guys that have been accused of making a good living out of turning up on film sets and simply reading out their lines. Think about it, though. If you were an actor, what would you prefer to do? Create a character who bears little relation to yourself and who you can leave behind once you've finished the picture, or play yourself and so have your every neurosis, flaw and fear played out on a screen seventy feet wide for millions of people to see? In an art form as unforgiving as cinema, the brave man is the one who shares his soul with the world.

The fact that, in my years of watching Steve McQueen, I've rarely been distracted or embarrassed by his performances (only his cracks at comedy are truly cringe-inducing) suggests to me that he was a pretty fine screen actor. When I watch his films, I don't keep thinking to myself; 'That's Steve McQueen.' To be honest, I don't think of much at all. I just find myself swept along with the journeys his characters undertake. A lot of people say that McQueen was one of the guys who only ever played himself. These critics clearly forget that Steve trained under the legendary Lee Strasberg. But even if Steve McQueen did only ever play Steve McQueen on camera, you only have to consider what a contradictory character he was, how he was by turns fearless, dumb, cowardly, smart, monstrous, compassionate, brutal and admirable, to realise that his decision to share himself with cinema audiences was one that should leave us feeling privileged rather than short changed.

Richard Luck
(Welwyn Garden City, April 2000)

Steve McQueen: So Tough

"I live for myself and I answer to nobody."

Every film fan can recall the moment when they realised that movies were a pretty cool thing to be interested in. As a supposedly serious film writer, my epiphany ought to have occurred during something profound like the Odessa Steps sequence from *Battleship Potemkin* or the awesome, 'Rosebud'-revealing climax of *Citizen Kane*, but it didn't. No, for me, the first time films became something more than moving wallpaper was the first time I saw Steve McQueen speeding towards the Swiss border on a motorcycle being chased by what looked like the entire Third Reich in *The Great Escape*.

McQueen's amazing bike chase is the sort of ludicrous, filmstealing moment that appears on few actors' CVs. Even really big stars don't often get the opportunity to do something so effortlessly cool and iconic. What makes McQueen's filmography so remarkable is that he had status-establishing incidents in virtually all of the films he made. The car chase in *Bullitt*, the chess scene seduction in *The Thomas Crown Affair*, the "we deal in lead, friend" line in *The Magnificent Seven*, practically every scene in *The Getaway*. McQueen's career was a veritable cutting book of classic scenes.

'The King of Cool' was, in fact, one of the many titles Steve McQueen had to shoulder during his short life. 'Arch-chauvinist.' 'Limited actor.' 'The new Paul Newman.' He was lumbered with each of these epithets at one time or another. While some of the titles were accurate (McQueen actively pursued Newman's crown and made no secret of his dislike of feminism) and others were downright unfair (within his range, Hollywood had never produced a talent to rival him), it was McQueen's coolness that the papers would always refer back to. Even today, almost twenty years after his death, it's the Rolex-wearing, fast-car driving McQueen that biographers marvel over and advertisers exploit. Hipness has guaranteed Steve McQueen a place in Hollywood's Hall of Fame but it has also distracted people from his very real talents and from his true status, not as a phantom of fashion, but as a king of genuine courage.

"I'm out of the Midwest. It was a good place to come from. It gives you a sense of right or wrong and fairness, which is lacking in our society."

Terrence Steven McQueen was born on 24 March 1930 in Beech Grove, Indiana, his name the only gift from a father he never knew. Years later, McQueen would reminisce about the "good grounding" and "strong values" that his Mid-Western upbringing had given him. The reality, however, was far less romantic. A gang member from the moment he could walk, the young Steve seemed set for a career as a petty thief and vandal until one run-in too many with the law led to him being sentenced to the infamous Boys Republic reform school in Chino, California. Scared straight during his eighteen months there, he left a semi-reformed character and promptly enlisted in the United States Marine Corps. Since he was already a big fan of bikes and motor vehicles, McQueen enjoyed his duties as a mechanic and tank driver but continued to have trouble with authority figures. So it was that after three years service he received an honourable discharge and, after drifting around the States and the Caribbean, settled in New York, taking on a hundred and one different jobs to pursue his two new loves: acting and motorcycles.

No one's quite sure how and why the tough, masculine McQueen fell in love with the relatively effete world of acting. A way to meet women? A step up from his previous careers as a circus barker and Cuban brothel 'bouncer'? Both are possible explanations. More convincing than either, however, is an apparent realisation on McQueen's behalf that his colourful youth had provided him with experiences that could usefully inform his performances. Whatever the real reason for Steve taking to the boards, it wasn't long before theatre school and off-Broadway productions transformed into television contracts.

The gigs were small to begin with: an uncredited role in the Paul Newman vehicle *Somebody Up There Likes Me*; minor parts in *Goodyear Television Playhouse* productions; and underwhelming Westerns. It wasn't financially rewarding work but it provided McQueen with enough exposure to land the role of Josh Randall in the TV horse opera *Wanted: Dead Or Alive*. The show that did for McQueen what *Rawhide* would do for Clint Eastwood, it eventually came off air in 1961, by which time Steve had starred in *The Magnificent Seven* and become a bona fide film celebrity.

From here, his rise to high estate was rapid. In 1963, less than fifteen years after he'd taken up acting, he was billed ahead of Richard Attenborough, James Garner and *Magnificent Seven* co-stars James Coburn and Charles Bronson in *The Great Escape*. Three years later, he was Oscar nominated for his bravura turn in war epic *The Sand Pebbles*. He did pretty well on the business front, too, setting up Solar, the production company behind hits like *Nevada Smith*, *The Thomas Crown Affair* and *Bullitt*. A second development deal with First Artists founders Barbra Streisand, Dustin Hoffman, Sidney Poitier and Paul Newman proved less fruitful but was a potent symbol of his star power. And then in 1974, eighteen years after appearing beside him unbilled, McQueen co-starred with Newman in *The Towering Inferno*, capping him in both the credit and capital stakes in the process. In terms of income, Steve had outstripped Newman years before. Indeed, with a salary of $5 million a movie, Steve McQueen was the highest paid actor in the world.

"I have to be careful because I'm a limited actor. I mean, my range isn't very great. There's a whole lot of stuff I can't do, so I have to find characters and situations that feel right. Even then, when I've got something that fits, it's a hell of a lot of work. I'm not a serious actor. There's something about my shaggy-dog eyes that makes people think I'm good. I'm not all that good."

Act, of course, is the one thing a lot of people claim McQueen couldn't do. Those that say this ignore the fact that Steve studied at the Neighbourhood Playhouse, won a scholarship to the prestigious Herbert-Bergoff Drama School and in 1955, he and Martin Landau (*Crimes & Misdemeanours*, *Ed Wood*, *Space 1999*) were the only two actors out of the 2,000 who auditioned to gain entrance to Lee Strasberg's Actors' Studio, a prestigious seat of learning whose graduates include Robert De Niro, Al Pacino, Marlon Brando and Marilyn Monroe.

All great actors have certain tricks that enable them to transform the vacuous into the compelling. Whenever Robert Redford wants to give the impression he is thinking, he rolls the food around his mouth when he eats. Jack Lemon, when he wants to register disgust, clamps a hand to his stomach as if he's about to be sick. And when Klaus Kinski wanted to suggest that he was as mad in front of the camera as he was behind it, he spiralled into shot.

Foremost amongst Steve McQueen's armoury was 'the smile,' so disarming that you imagine *Thomas Crown* co-star Faye Dunaway would have swooned even if the script hadn't told her to, and so winning that you really understand why Richard Attenborough and Gordon Jackson don't get too upset when they discover that that bloody tunnel is fifty feet too short. If the grin itself was good, it was all the better for being teamed with the only pair of eyes in Hollywood that were bluer than Paul Newman's.

Equally crucial to McQueen's popularity was his physique. At 5 feet 6 inches and 150 pounds, he was neither a tall nor thick set man. He wasn't particularly muscular either - a punishing, two-hours-a-day exercise regime left him looking more like a middle-distance runner than Charles Atlas. But just as the spindly Tom

Cruise gets more fan mail than Arnold Schwarzenneger (a man once described as having a body like a 'condom stuffed full of walnuts'), so McQueen's lean, hairless torso made him a much bigger sex symbol than the far brawnier Charles Bronson. (Bronson only became a true star when, aware that he couldn't compete with the muscle-bound action heroes of the mid-70s, he started to exude a brand of stealth and charm not unlike McQueen's.) Whatever it was that made his chest attractive, a top-off shot became a prerequisite for a McQueen movie.

Steve's willingness to take his kit off wasn't inspired by vanity. It was simply a case of someone playing to their strengths. In the same way he also learnt how to use the camera, not so much to make himself look good but to disguise his limitations. The quest to compensate for his lack of size and maximise his screen presence led to McQueen cultivating a shot that would appear in most of his films. It worked like this... The first image of Steve on screen would be a tight close-up of the back of his head emphasising the muscles in his neck and the broadness of his shoulders. He would then turn towards the camera, flashing either his smile or eyes or, better still, both. It was a simple shot but one that made McQueen look simultaneously strong and beautiful. What's more, when it took place on a screen some seventy feet wide and twenty four feet high, it left you in no doubt that Steve McQueen was a screen-filling talent.

The smile, the eyes, the body, the angles - they were McQueen's tools. If they were all he'd had at his disposal, he might still have become a leading actor, maybe even a star. That he became an icon stemmed in part from his understanding of acting in general and screen acting in particular. Thanks to his time on *Wanted: Dead Or Alive* and his appearances in a whole bunch of movies that nobody ever saw (*Never Love A Stranger*, *The Blob*, *The Great St Louis Bank Robbery*), he'd been able to work out that you have to do very little on camera to convey emotion (see McQueen's comedy performances to see how bad eye-rolling makes you look on screen). He must also have been aware that there are some guys who the camera simply loves and, since he was one of those lucky chaps, he really didn't need to twitch and squint to get attention. A willingness to listen and take advice didn't do McQueen any harm, either. Indeed, after John Sturges took him to one side on the set of *The Great Escape* and told him to react rather than act, his performances improved immeasurably. But as with all our favourite actors, there is also something else, an ingredient X that transforms the good into the great. In McQueen's case, it would appear to be the gift that John Travolta (who also possesses it) identified as the ability to convey a thought the moment it comes into the head. Unfortunately, Travolta has squandered his special power on ghastly baby talk movies and screen rot like *Phenomenon* and *Michael*. Steve McQueen, on the other hand, used his gift to make him a legend.

(It might have taken the 'serious' critics a while to wake up to his acting talent, but Steve's performances didn't go completely unrecognised. Beside his Oscar nomination for *The Sand Pebbles*, he received Golden Globe nods for *Pebbles*, *Papillon* and surprisingly, *The Reivers*. Outside of awards for performing, Steve won the World's Film Favourite Golden Globe in 1967 and 1970 and picked up Photoplay's Most Popular Male Star gong in 1968.)

The other key to Steve's megastardom was his identifying himself with a particular type of character: silent, actionful, alone. McQueen's preferred screen persona superficially sounds like every other film action hero. However, Steve was willing to do things on camera that Mel Gibson, Tom Cruise, Bruce Willis and the like would only rarely contemplate. For one thing, he was happy for his characters to die if the story called for it (*Hell Is For Heroes*, *Tom Horn*) and early in his career he'd even cry on camera (*The Great St Louis Bank Robbery*). For another, while they give the impression that they don't need anybody, some of his characters form genuine, life-enhancing friendships (Charrière's bond with Louis in *Papillon*, Hilts' relationship with Ives in *The Great Escape*, Vin's rapport with the rest of *The Magnificent Seven*). And while, as in real life, McQueen always gets the girl, the relationships are seldom smooth (*Love With The Proper Stranger*, *The Hunter*), occasionally violent (*Baby,The Rain Must Fall*, *The Get-*

away) and are sometimes dissolved by the time the movie ends (*The Cincinnati Kid*, *The Thomas Crown Affair*, *Junior Bonner*). In fact, the only thing Steve's screen incarnations have in common with the regular Hollywood action hero is that a lot of them ride off into the sunset (*The Magnificent Seven*, *The Thomas Crown Affair*, *The Getaway*), although even this movie cliché wasn't all it was cracked up to be in McQueen's hands as his characters sometimes disappear into uncertainty (*The Cincinnati Kid*, *Junior Bonner*, *Papillon*). So, while he will forever appear in lists of great Hollywood action heroes, Steve McQueen on camera wasn't quite like the other boys. He was a mixture of made man and misfit, ice-cool loner and lukewarm companion. He was, in fact, very much like the real Steve McQueen.

"They call me a chauvinist pig - I am and I don't give a damn!"

There's no disputing the paradoxical nature of Steve McQueen. He was a lousy husband (the only one of his three wives he didn't cheat on was number three, Barbara Minty, and that was probably because he was too sick) but he was also an excellent father. He liked to be thought of as a man completely in control of his destiny but he was a slave to tarot cards and horoscopes (alarmed to hear that satanic rituals had been held outside his Palm Springs ranch, he consulted a psychic who warned him that these 'witches' were: "praying for your death. They are concentrating that you should die at your own hand. They would like you to get further into drugs. They would like for you to begin racing cars. Whatever you do, don't get into any cars that are a combination of red and black." From that day on, Steve never raced red or black autos). And while he courted the image of a loner, he built up a team of artists and technicians that he worked with time and again: directors Sam Peckinpah, John Sturges, Norman Jewison, Robert Wise and Robert Mulligan; personal manager Hillard Elkins; producers and Solar associates Jack N Reddish and Robert E Relyea; actors Robert Vaughn, Don Gordon, Vic Tayback, Dub Taylor and Paul Fix; cinematographer Fred Koenekamp; writer/assistant director Walter Hill; designer Theadora Van Runckle; composer Lalo Schifrin; and stuntmen Bud Ekins, Carey Loftin and Loren Janes.

By far the most unattractive aspect of the many-faced McQueen was his sexism and homophobia. The latter seemed to have its origins in the rumour that was spread around Hollywood in the mid-60s that Steve's marriage was a sham and he was actually homosexual. The former had a lot to do with the age in which McQueen was raised and the fact that, as a Marine, movie star and motor-racing driver, he'd spent his life working in three of the world's most sexist professions.

As unattractive as his attitudes were, I don't think they should pose a barrier to saluting McQueen. We now live in an age when, the moment we discover anything unappetising about one of our heroes, we turn on them as if they were Oswald Moseley. So what if Martin Luther King was a serial adulterer or Winston Churchill was a racist or David Bowie once said that what this country needs it a good fascist dictatorship? At the end of the day wouldn't you rather have Steve McQueen, a sexist dinosaur but a great star, than, say, pussy-whipped Ethan Hawke. At least ex-Marine McQueen suggested he might actually be able to pull off the same stuff his characters did. You cannot say the same for the current generation of leading men - pudgy Matt Damon, ladyboy Leonardo DiCaprio or lissom Jude Law.

"Stardom equals freedom. It's the only equation that matters."

And even if you are of the opinion that Steve was the world's worst gay-baiting homophobe, it's hard not to be impressed by the McQueen catalogue of cool.

i) He received martial arts tuition from Bruce Lee and Chuck Norris. Indeed, for a couple of years Steve trained in the same dojo as Norris, The Dragon and James Coburn - they must have had a hell of job getting all of their egos into the room simultaneously. There has been a lot of speculation over exactly how good McQueen was at either Karate or jeet kune do, Lee's specially devised discipline. The uncertainty stems from the fact that, since he didn't want his expertise used against him should he ever be sued, McQueen never studied for belts (he never used his skills on screen either although he did talk about making a martial arts documentary, provisionally titled *Mind Like Water*). In lieu of recognised ranking, we'll just have to accept the opinion of Chuck Norris who thought Steve possessed the skills and discipline of a third dan black belt. As for McQueen's relationship with Bruce Lee, it soured after Steve learned that the martial artist had received $3 million to star in *Enter The Dragon* (1973, dir Robert Clouse). McQueen, by contrast, had earned a paltry $2 million for starring in *Papillon*. Although their friendship fell apart, Steve, Coburn and Norris served as pall-bearers at Lee's Seattle funeral.

ii) He was a successful motor-racing driver. Steve owned cars, bikes and airplanes and could propel all at truly frightening speeds (he drove a terrified Bruce Lee through the tight curves of Mulholland Drive at 140mph and was kicked out of the Carnegie Technical Institute for riding his motorbike up and down the corridors). His professional achievements included patenting a racing car seat, taking Mario Andretti to the limit in the Sebring International Twelve Hour Endurance Race, representing Team USA at the International Six Day Trials in East Germany and appearing on the cover of Sports Illustrated in 1971. While it has been suggested that Steve's success owed more to bloody-mindedness than genuine talent, he was certainly a lot more comfortable behind the wheel than that bloke out of Boyzone who keeps crashing (see also the chapter Silver Dream McQueen).

iii) He was stalked by Charles Manson. More to the point, had he not been on a date with one of his women, McQueen would have been at 10050 Cielo Drive when The Family murdered Sharon Tate (aka Mrs Roman Polanski), her unborn son Paul Richard Polanski and their friends Abigail Folger, Voytek Frykowski and celebrity hairdresser Jay Sebring. Not content with calling himself Jesus, auditioning for The Monkees, hanging out with The Beach Boys and finding apocalyptic messages in The Beatles' *White Album*, Manson had made McQueen number one on his celebrity hit list (other Family targets included Richard Burton, Elizabeth Taylor, Frank Sinatra and, rather surprisingly, Tom Jones). Despite the arrest and successful prosecution of Manson and his cronies, Steve never again left the house without a loaded revolver in his car's glove compartment. And what had McQueen done to incur 'Jesus Christ's' wrath? He failed to commission a script Manson had sent to Solar pictures in 1968. Incidentally, Steve wasn't the only person whom good fortune saved from The Family. Also invited but unable to attend Tate's soirée were Jeremy Lloyd, one-time husband of Joanna Lumley and co-creator of Brit sitcom *Are You Being Served?,* and author Jerzy Kosinski (*Being There*) who used the killings as the basis for his novel *Blind Fate.* As for the way Manson planned to kill McQueen, it was as the psychic had predicted - 'at his own hands.'

iv) He slept with the entire world. Steve dated some of the most beautiful women in Hollywood. His list of conquests included *Cincinnati Kid* co-star Ann-Margret, 'sock-it-to-me girl' Judy Carne, Jacqueline Bisset (his *Bullitt* love interest), Mamie Van Doren, the aforementioned Sharon Tate (who he'd met on the set of *Soldier In The Rain* and wanted cast in *The Cincinnati Kid*) and *Thomas Crown*'s Faye Dunaway. His seduction of Ali McGraw is particularly legendary since a) it occurred while the pair were shooting *The Getaway* and b) it took place right under the nose of McGraw's husband, *The Godfather/Chinatown/Rosemary's Baby* producer Robert Evans. Although forged in intense circumstances, McGraw and McQueen's relationship, nevertheless, lasted seven years together. (Don't feel too sorry for raving egomaniac Evans, mind. As Paramount President Frank Yablans told Peter Biskind in *Easy Riders, Raging Bulls*; "Evans pushed them together. He created the break-up with Ali, the public cuckolding. 'Bob, you're going to lose your wife. These two are going at it hot and heavy.' 'It's just a passing thing.' He didn't give a shit. It didn't matter to him. He's a very strange man. He couldn't be married, couldn't live a normal sane life. He drove her out.")

v) His drugs intake was what Terrence McKenna would describe as 'heroic.' We're not just talking beer, whisky, tobacco and marijuana, either. At the height of his fame, Steve was using LSD to expand his mind and amyl nitrate to expand his underpants. He also took cocaine which almost cost him his life when, in 1970, he took a couple of friends for a spin around the Le Mans circuit while high. The car crashed, the passengers were hospitalised and the incident was hushed up until after Steve's death.

vi) He was a fully qualified stuntman. Contrary to popular belief Steve didn't perform the motorcycle leap in *The Great Escape* nor most of the stunt driving in *Bullitt* (on the *Johnny Carson Tonight Show*, Steve openly admitted that his friend Bud Ekins had jumped the barbwire fence). He did, however, do all the bull riding, bronco bustin' and calf wrestlin' in *Junior Bonner* and was made an honorary member of the Stuntman's Association Of Motion Pictures in 1977. As for his equestrian skills, *Tom Horn* cinematographer John A Alonzo recalls that: "I've never seen anyone handle a horse better. He would get on Buster with a rifle and fire at full gallop. He was going as fast as the horse could go and he handled it beautifully." (McQueen had overcome his fear of horses and his inability to ride to get the role of Josh Randall in *Wanted: Dead Or Alive.*)

vii) He made President Richard Nixon's infamous 'Enemies' list. The government started to pursue Steve after he intimated that he would participate in Martin Luther King's 1963 Washington march (in the end, McQueen couldn't attend but he fully endorsed the good Doctor's work). Throughout the rest of his career, he was the subject of countless FBI reports and was closely scrutinised by the paranoid Nixon. It's hard to know quite why McQueen was considered so suspicious, although his popularity in Eastern Europe in general and Russia in particular might provide some explanation.

viii) He was a fashion guru. McQueen's style coups included having a Rolex named after him (The Rolex Explorer II [ref. 1655] is officially known as the 'McQueen Rolex') and making the Heuer Monaco wristwatch which he sported in *Le Mans* so popular that it was re-released in the 1990s (Giovanni Ribisi's crooked dealer wears one in Ben Younger's *Boiler Room*). Steve was also the first man ever to appear on the cover of *Harper's Bazaar*. While his contract allowed him to keep the Italian suits he wore in *The Thomas Crown Affair*, Steve's favourite outfit remained one he'd been wearing since long time before he arrived in Hollywood - T-shirt and jeans.

"I believe in me. I'm a little screwed up but I'm beautiful."

And then there is the McQueen legacy: his two children. Terri Leslie tragically succumbed to liver cancer after putting up the sort of fight that her father would have been proud. Chad(wick) Steven carved out a career as an actor, producer and stuntman in spite of the pressure of having every exec in the world say to him: 'I loved your Dad in *The Getaway/Bullit/The Magnificent Seven* etc.'

Compared to some of his contemporaries (Paul Newman, Yul Brynner, James Coburn, Charles Bronson), McQueen's filmography is incredibly short (just 27 films in a 22-year career). And as for his canon of quality pictures, well, it's positively puny. It is perhaps for this reason that critics and fans have a tendency to dwell upon the pictures McQueen didn't make. He chose not to appear in *Ocean's Eleven*, *Dirty Harry*, *The French Connection* and *Ice Station Zebra*. He wasn't allowed to star in *Breakfast At Tiffany's* because *Wanted: Dead Or Alive* wouldn't release him. He was kicked off *Butch Cassidy & The Sundance Kid* because Paul Newman was worried that Steve would upstage him. And he simply didn't live to make *Hang Tough*, Aussie Western *Quigley Down Under* and motorcycle drama *The Last Ride*.

While a third of his films are almost unwatchable and only half of his movies are any good, Steve McQueen made enough excellent pictures for us to overlook his unrealised work. Indeed, besides his pretty decent films (*The Sand Pebbles*, *The Thomas Crown Affair*, *Love With The Proper Stranger*, *The Towering Inferno*, *The Cincinnati Kid*), Steve made three films that would appear on any list of classic films from the 60s (*The Magnificent Seven*, *The Great Escape*, *Bullitt*) and another three that would have to appear on a similar survey of 70s cinema (*Junior Bonner*, *The Getaway*, *Papillon*). Steve wasn't only good when surrounded by the likes of Richard Attenborough, Yul Brynner, Robert Preston and Ben Johnson, however. Even when the films were crap, McQueen could be red hot. And while pictures like *The War Lover*, *Nevada Smith* and *Tom Horn* are part of the reason McQueen's work has never been taken seriously it is, ironically, Steve's superior acting in sub-standard movies and in poor company that marks him out as a truly great acting talent.

Twenty years after his death, Steve McQueen is still a part of our lives. In the month that this book was put to bed, a horse called Papillon won The Martell Grand National at Aintree, the news broke that Hitler himself had ordered that 50 of the 'Great Escape' POWs be shot (no points for guessing which film clips were used to illustrate that story), and the *Bullitt*-inspired Ford Puma advertisement began to air again. The commercial, created by Young & Rubicam, is a real piece of work. The special effects used to lift shots of McQueen out of Peter Yates' cop classic are impressive enough in themselves. But the CGI alone can't explain why the advertisement works so well. No, that has a lot to do with the star. As Y&R's Paul Venn explains; "we were looking for a spokesman who could represent the Puma's character. The exhilarating drive, the true style, the daring personality. All the research groups we held told us that McQueen possessed those characteristics." Or to quote Pete Smith, managing director of Virnwood Ford in Dorset; "It's a bloody great piece of advertising. No other actor would have worked. I mean, who is there these days? They're all a load of poofs, this new lot. A load of woollies! There's no one as good as McQueen!"

I think that says it all, really.

Small Screen Success & Big Screen Debuts

Steve McQueen is unusual amongst actors in that he made his 'unofficial' big-screen debut before he'd appeared on either the Broadway stage or network television.

Somebody Up There Likes Me (1956)

Cast: Paul Newman (Rocky Graziano), Pier Angeli (Norma), Everett Sloane (Irving Cohen), Eileen Heckart (Ma Barbella), Sal Mineo (Romolo), Harold J Stone (Nick Barbella), Joseph Buloff (Benny), Sammy White (Whitey Brimstein), Arch Johnson (Heldon), Robert Lieb (Questioner), Theodore Newton (Eddie Eagen), Caswell Adams (Sam, uncredited), Frank Campanella (Detective, uncredited), Walter Cartier (Polack, uncredited), Angela Cartwright (Audrey aged three, uncredited), Russ Conway (Captain Grifton, uncredited), Clancy Cooper (Captain Lancheck, uncredited), Michael Dante (Shorty, uncredited), Robert Easton (Corporal Quinbury, uncredited), John Eldredge (Warden Niles, uncredited), Jan Gillum

(Yolanda aged 12, uncredited), Charles Green (Curtis Hughtower, uncredited), Donna Jo Gribble (Yolanda Barbella, uncredited), Dean Jones (Private, uncredited), Jackie Kelk (George, uncredited), David Leonard (Mr Mueller, uncredited), Robert Loggia (Frankie Preppo, uncredited), Steve McQueen (Fido aka Fidel aka Street Hood, uncredited), Judson Pratt (Johnny Hyland, uncredited), Matt Crowley (Lou Stillman, uncredited), Harry Wismer and Sam Taub (Announcers, uncredited), Terry Rangno (Rocky aged eight, uncredited), Court Shepard (Tony Zale, uncredited), Ray Stricklyn (Bryson, uncredited), James Todd (Colonel, uncredited), Ray Walker (ring announcer, uncredited)

Crew: Director Robert Wise, Writer Ernest Lehman, Autobiography Rocky Graziano, Producer Charles Schnee, Associate Producer James E Newcom, Music Bronislau Kaper, Cinematographer Joseph Ruttenberg, Editor Albert Akst, Art Directors Cedric Gibbons & Malcolm Brown, Technical Advisor Johnny Indrisano, 110 minutes

Story: Rebel teen Rocky Graziano is caught committing petty crimes on the streets of New York. Sent to reform school, he later joins the Army but is dishonourably discharged. A spell in Leavenworth Prison follows, during which fitness instructor Johnny Hyland spies Rocky's boxing potential. A free man again, Rocky hooks up with manager Irving Cohen and hits the fight circuit. Alas the boxing world is as corrupt and without honour as the life of crime Rocky used to lead. Graziano doesn't feel like anything more than a paid thug until he falls in love with Norma. With new meaning and direction in his life, Rocky strives for self-respect and sporting triumph. Defeated by middleweight champion Tony Zale, he secures a rematch only for ex-inmate Frankie Peppo to crawl out of the woodwork and threaten to expose Rocky's past unless he throws a fight. When Rocky calls off the bout, his past is revealed and his license to fight in New York state is revoked. He eventually gets another crack at Zale in Chicago and wins out in a brutal, bloody clash.. As he returns home to New York, Rocky remembers his good fortune rather than his bad luck. His story serves to prove how people can rise above adversity.

McQueen Off-Screen: The most famous behind-the-scenes story about *Somebody Up There Likes Me* concerns the fact that Rocky Graziano was originally going to be played by James Dean. As for Steve's involvement in the picture, that was entirely down to Robert Wise liking the young actor's cockiness. Remembers the director, "he walked in for the audition wearing a beanie hat and that smile and within a few minutes, he'd got the part."

McQueen On-Screen: Playing a street kid who steals hubcaps, picks fights and plays pool, Steve's first film role didn't make huge demands of him. What the part did do was to give McQueen his first valuable lessons in acting for the cameras. What's more, Steve's very first moment on celluloid (Fido wheels away from the pool table at which he is playing, pulls a knife, realises that the man who surprised him is his friend Rocky and breaks into a huge grin) features what were to become two of his on-screen trademarks, the 'behind the shoulders' shot and the Cheshire Cat smile. While a small, uncredited performance didn't make for the best first entry on a CV, Steve really couldn't have asked for a better debut scene.

McQueen's Confederates: Somebody Up There Likes Me threw Steve straight into the mix with two men who would have a remarkable impact on his career, Robert Wise and Paul Newman. Just over a decade after shooting *Somebody...*, Wise would direct McQueen in *The Sand Pebbles* to his sole Oscar nomination. Newman, meanwhile, was the actor whose success Steve was determined to emulate. The next time the two appeared on screen together, in the action epic *The Towering Inferno*, McQueen was as big a star and every bit as well paid as his idol.

McQueen's Cash: Steve was paid a princely $50 a day. He was originally down to get $19, but a close-up and a couple of lines doubled his salary.

The Verdict: Robert Wise's best film after *The Haunting*, it would be nice to attribute more of *Somebody Up There Likes Me*'s artistic success to Steve. Unfortunately, McQueen's performance isn't really long enough to rate. And since *Somebody...* isn't really a McQueen movie, I don't want to discuss it in too much depth. However, for Newman's punchy performance alone, the picture deserves 4/5.

It was after finishing *Somebody...* that Steve starred in Broadway productions of *Hatful Of Rain* and *Two Fingers Of Pride* and started to make his first serious money from acting (he'd previously only appeared in a few plays in upstate New York). As at home in

23

the Big Apple as he was on stage, it must have come as a big blow to Steve when his girlfriend Neile was offered a role in the motion picture *This Could Be The Night* and the couple were forced to relocate to California.

While Neile made her movie, McQueen set out to find work on the small screen. He made his television debut in 'The Shrivington Raiders' instalment of *The Philco-Goodyear Hour* and went on to appear in episodes of *The United States Steel Hour*, *Armstrong Circle Theatre*, *Wells Fargo* (the writers included David Samuel Peckinpah), *West Point* and *Studio One* (in a production of Reginald (*Twelve Angry Men*) Rose's two-hander *The Defender*). In between his bits and pieces of TV work, Steve found time to make his first properly billed film appearance.

Never Love A Stranger (1958)

Cast: John Drew Barrymore (Frankie Kane), Lita Milan (Julie), Robert Bray ('Silk' Fennelli), Steve McQueen (Martin Cabell), Salem Ludwig (Moishe Moscowitz), R G Armstrong (Flix), Douglas Fletcher Rodgers (Brother Bernard), Felice Orlandi (Bert)

Crew: Director Robert Stevens, Writer & Novel Harold Robbins, Producers Harold Robbins & Richard Day, Music Raymond Scott, Cinematographer Lee Garmes, Editor Sidney Katz, Art Director Leo Kerz, 93 minutes

Story: School friends Frankie Kane and Martin Cabell grow up to become a gangster and an assistant district attorney, respectively. In spite of their different lifestyle choices, the two remain friends and team up to track down a vicious hood. From the pen of Harold Robbins, a story of no-good gangsters, drop-dead gorgeous gals and sordid intrigue.

McQueen Off-Screen: Steve chalked up his first official off-screen affair during the filming of *Never Love A Stranger*. He'd been married a full eight months.

Author Harold Robbins also penned *The Carpetbaggers,* a trashy best-seller which featured a character called Nevada Smith, more of whom later.

Never Love A Stranger only received a limited release in America because some States objected to its pro-Jewish stance. That's

America, the land of the free, in case you were getting it confused with some unfamiliar totalitarian nation.

McQueen On-Screen: Steve's range might not have been as limited as either he or many of his critics thought it was, but there was no way the Roman Catholic-raised McQueen could nail Martin Cabell, a Hasidic District Attorney who is stunned to find out that his childhood friend isn't a Catholic. Critics at the time described him as looking like a cross between a Botticelli angel and a chimpanzee.

McQueen's Confederates: Although Steve never again worked with any of his co-stars, R G Armstrong was part of Sam Peckinpah's stock company, an elite group of talents to which McQueen was admitted in the early 70s.

McQueen's Cash: Steve was offered $3,000 or a percentage of the film's profits. Ever the shrewd businessman, McQueen saw *Never Love A Stranger* for the dog it was and took the money.

The Verdict: Not much to say really - Steve doesn't make for the world's most convincing Jewish attorney and *Never Love A Stranger* doesn't make for the most convincing screen drama ever shot. Film 2/5, McQueen 2/5.

Shortly before *Never Love A Stranger* came along, Steve appeared as lawman Josh Randall in an episode of the Western series *Trackdown,* entitled 'The Bounty Hunter.' Shortly afterwards, *Trackdown* was thrown onto the TV scrap pile. The execs, however, had been so impressed with McQueen's likeable gunman that they gave him his own series, *Wanted: Dead Or Alive*.

Make no mistake about it, *Wanted: Dead Or Alive* wasn't one of *the* great TV Western series. It certainly wasn't a patch on Peckinpah's *Rifleman* or *The Westerner.* In truth, it wasn't a whole lot more demanding than *Champion The Wonder Horse*. Admittedly, Randall's character did have an edge: his rifle ('the mare's leg') wasn't the standard sheriff's longarm but a nasty, lead-shot spraying, sawn-off number. But *Wanted: Dead Or Alive* wasn't really interested in portraying the West as it really was. It was about delivering darn-tootin' action every Saturday night and placating the sponsors, Viceroy 'The Thinking Man's Cigarette.' There was certainly no disputing the show's success. First airing in August 1958, *Wanted: Dead Or Alive* ran for 117 episodes, making its producer Vincent Fennely wealthy beyond his dreams and making Steve McQueen as familiar a household name as Coca-Cola. If you want to see what all the fuss was about, colourised instalments still occasionally air on British commercial television.

When he wasn't riding the High Sierras as Josh Randall, Steve starred in the *Alfred Hitchcock Presents...* episodes, 'Human Interest Story' (opposite his wife) and 'Man Of The South,' which 'inspired' Quentin Tarantino's contribution to the portmanteau film *Four Rooms*. McQueen also fitted in a string of movies appearances around his TV schedule, beginning with a sci-fi picture that could kindly be described as appalling. It was a film that critics, fans and even McQueen himself would erroneously refer to as his first.

The Blob (1958)

Cast: Steven McQueen (Steve Andrews), Aneta Corsaut (Jane Martin), Earl Rowe (Police Lieutenant Dave), Olin Howlin (Old Man), Steven Chase (Dr T Hallen), John Benson (Sergeant Jim Bert), George Karas (Officer Ritchie), Lee Paton (Kate The Nurse), Elbert Smith (Henry Martin), Vince Barni (George The Café Owner), Audrey Metcalf (Elizabeth Martin), Jasper Deeter (Civil Defence Volunteer), Elinor Hammer (Mrs Porter), Pamela Curran (Smooching Teenager), Julie Cousins (Sally The Waitress), Keith Almoney (Danny Martin), Robert Fields (Tony Gressette), James Bonnet (Mooch Miller), Anthony Franke (Al), Molly Ann Bourne & Diane Tabben (Teenagers)

Crew: Director Irvin S Yeaworth Jnr, Writers Theodore Simonson & Kate Phillips, Story Irvine H Millgate, Producer Jack H Harris, Associate Producer Russell Doughten, Music Ralph Carmichael, Title Song Burt Bacharach & Hal David, Cinematographer Thomas Spalding, Editor Alfred Hillmann, Art Directors William Jersey & Karl Karlson, Special Effects Barton Sloane, 85 minutes

Story: The 1950s. Small town America. Teenagers necking. Spaceship lands. Marauding alien creature rendered using piss-poor special effects emerges. Teenagers run to tell their parents. Parents don't listen. Creature marauds unconvincingly through the town. Someone actually says "has everyone in this fool town gone crazy?" Seemingly invulnerable alien turns out to have a rather weedy weakness. The creature is iced, literally. The whole town parties down. Believe me, even if you haven't seen this movie, you have seen this movie.

McQueen Off-Screen: In Marshall Terrill's *Steve McQueen: Portrait Of An American Rebel*, *Blob* producer Jack Harris recalls that even back in 1958, Steve could be a gigantic pain in the arse. "He had a reputation for being a troublemaker and he earned it sincerely. Whenever we had a problem, the director would call me and say, "well, your star is acting up again." And I'd run down to the set and sit down with Steve and once I got past the 'I'm going to call my agent, I'm going to call my manager, I'm going to call my lawyer' routine, we were able to talk out what was wrong."

McQueen On-Screen: Too old to be playing a teenager at 28, Steve (billed as Steven, presumably because his mother was working in the publicity department) gives a wide-eyed, wide-mouthed performance of the sort familiar to fans of Roger Corman's movies. The Blob, on the other hand, is a superb, charismatic player and it's a shame that his screen outings have been restricted to *Beware! The Blob* (aka *Son Of The Blob*). While McQueen delivers a shockingly bad performance, it's worth noting that the film opens with his favourite 'over the shoulder' establishing shot. 13 years later, *Le Mans* would begin with the exact same image.

McQueen's Confederates: It's no surprise that once *The Blob* was over, Steve never wanted to see either his co-stars or the crew ever again. He wasn't the only one to distance himself from the project. You don't hear Burt Bacharach building the theme from *The Blob* into many of 'here's-one-you-might-remember' medleys, now do you?

McQueen's Cash: A princely $3,000. Amazingly, had Steve taken the 15% participation option he was offered, he would have become a millionaire many times over. Not that McQueen would be too pissed off - by the time the sequel to *The Blob* was made in 1971, he could demand $2 million a picture.

The Verdict: Like *Plan 9 From Outer Space, Teenage Caveman* and *The Viking Women & The Sea Serpent*, *The Blob* is huge fun but for reasons that were never intended. Film 1/5, McQueen 1/5.

The Great St Louis Bank Robbery (1959)

Cast: Steve McQueen (George Fowler), David Clarke (Gino), Crahan Denton (John Egan), Molly McCarthy (Ann), James Dukas (Willie), The Men Of The St Louis Police Department (Themselves)

Crew: Directors Charles Guggenheim & John Stix, Writer Richard T Heffron, Producer Charles Guggenheim, Associate Producer Richard T Heffron, Music Bernado Segall, Cinematographer Victor Duncan, Editor Warren Adams, 86 minutes

Also Known As: The St Louis Bank Robbery

Story: For the first time ever on the big screen: crime as it really is! See how a robbery is planned and executed! Gasp as a gang of hard-nosed crooks are exposed as a band of mother-fixated, homosexual losers. Smile as the fine men of the St Louis Police Department despatch three of the robbers before bringing getaway driver George Fowler to book! Laugh at the captured man's tears! And then go to bed thanking yourself you live in the land of the free, a country where truth and justice always prevail and a film featuring a Jewish attorney couldn't get distribution in 13 states!

McQueen Off-Screen: *The Great St Louis Bank Robbery* was a significant film for Steve McQueen if only because, for the first time ever, his name was billed above the movie.

McQueen On-Screen: It's not surprising Steve was drawn to the part of getaway driver George Fowler. An existential lover with a love of fast cars and hard crime, an ex-sports star who'd run away and joined the army to escape disgrace - there was a lot about the part that Steve either was or would have liked to have been. However, if *The Great St Louis Bank Robbery* is remembered for anything, it is for the finale in which - shock, horror! - STEVE McQUEEN CRIES! Real tears and everything!

McQueen's Confederates: Steve was too busy juggling his TV and film careers to develop any on-set friendships.

McQueen Quotes: George Fowler: "They come around and they promise you everything. They keep you in college because you can do something well. One mistake and you find out you're just hired help!"

McQueen's Cash: $4,000. At the same time, Steve's wife Neile was earning over $40,000 a year as a dancer, model and actress.

You can imagine the mucho macho McQueen didn't take at all well to his wife being the leading breadwinner in his household. Fortunately for Steve's ego, his *Wanted: Dead Or Alive* salary would soon swell to $100,000 per annum.

The Verdict: The Great St Louis Bank Robbery isn't bad as B-movies go (the scenes in which the robbery is planned are particularly strong), but Steve McQueen as a blubbering bank robber isn't a becoming sight and it's one that sensitive children and fans of McQueen's later work should be spared. Film 3/5, McQueen 2/5.

Never So Few (1959)

Cast: Frank Sinatra (Tom C Reynolds), Gina Lollobrigida (Carla Vesari), Peter Lawford (Captain Grey Travis), Steve McQueen (Sergeant Bill Ringa), Richard Johnson (Captain Danny De Mortimer), Paul Henreid (Nikko Regas), Brian Donlevy (General Sloan), Dean Jones (Sergeant Jim Norby), Charles Bronson (Sergeant John Danforth), Philip Ahn (Nautaung), Robert Bray (Colonel Fred Parkson), Kipp Hamilton (Margaret Fitch), John Hoyt (Colonel Reed), Whit Bissell (Captain Alofson), Richard Lupino (Mike Island), Aki Aleong (Billingsly), Ross Elliott (Dr Barry, uncredited), James Hong (Ambassador, uncredited), Leon Lontoc (Laurel, uncredited), George Takei (Soldier In Hospital, uncredited)
Crew: Director John Sturges, Writer Millard Kaufman, Novel Tom T Chamales, Producer Edmund Grainger, Music Hugo Friedhofer, Cinematographer William H Daniels, Editor Ferris Webster, Art Directors Hans Peters & Addison Hehr, 124 minutes

Story: World War II, Burma and 400,000 rampaging Japanese soldiers are held back by 600 Kachin guerrillas, lead by an American army officer who looks a hell of a lot like Frank Sinatra. Based on a true story.

McQueen Off-Screen: It's hard to imagine but the part played by Steve McQueen in *Never So Few* was actually intended for Sammy Davis Jnr. Since it was designed as a comeback vehicle for Frank Sinatra's close friend Peter Lawford, the Chairman Of The Board saw no reason why there shouldn't be a part in the picture for his other Rat Pack pal. After all, at the time *Never So Few* was being put together, Davis was in debt to the tune of $300,000. No sooner had he secured the role than Davis gave an ill-advised radio interview. "I love Frank," the cocky song-and-dance man confessed, "and he was the kindest man in the world to me when I lost my eye in an auto accident and wanted to kill myself. But there are many things he does that there are no excuses for. Talent is not an excuse for bad manners. I don't care if you are the most talented person in the world. It does not give you the right to step on people and treat them rotten. This is what he does occasionally." Sinatra heard the interview, fired Sammy Davis and told director John Sturges to hire any young stud he wanted. A regular viewer of *Wanted: Dead Or Alive*, Sturges got on the phone to Steve McQueen's agent.

McQueen On-Screen: By far the most eye-catching thing about Steve's performance in *Never So Few* is the way in which he completely steals the scenes he shares with Frank Sinatra. I've always been a big fan of Sinatra the actor (*The Man With The Golden Arm*, *The Manchurian Candidate* and *High Society* all rank highly on my personal top 100 list). Good as he was, Ol' Blue Eyes only exuded star quality when a film was entirely about him (*Some Came Running*). The rest of the time, he was just a really great character actor. On the other hand, Steve McQueen, now that *Wanted: Dead Or Alive* had taught him how to play to the cameras, just had to hang around in front of the camera and let it fall in love with him. That was the difference - Sinatra was a star when the billing told people he was. Steve McQueen could be a star whenever he pleased.

McQueen's Confederates: Never So Few introduced Steve to the man who could take the most credit for making him a star, director John Sturges. The creator of classics like *Bad Day At Black Rock, Gunfight At The OK Corral* and *Last Train From Gun Hill*, Sturges combined an understanding of acting and intelligent drama that made him the sort of film-maker any young actor would want to work with. Sturges also introduced Steve to his assistant director and sometime assistant producer Robert Relyea, with whom McQueen would form a close professional relationship, and ex-coal miner Charles Bronson (né Buchinski), who would co-star with McQueen in the director's next picture.

Contrary to what's been written elsewhere, McQueen actually got on very well with Sinatra. The Chairman even offered Steve the lead in a film he planned to direct, *The Execution Of Private Slovik*. Since he wanted to be a star rather than a member of The Rat Pack, McQueen politely declined.

As for the other players, George Takei would use his uncredited turn as 'Soldier In Hospital' as a springboard to a lengthy career on board the Starship Enterprise. Dean Jones, on the other hand, would become famous as the man behind the wheel of Herbie, the VW Beetle with a mind of its own.

McQueen's Cash: $75,000 - real money at last!

The Verdict: Since the British did the bulk of the fighting during the Burma campaign, *Never So Few* is probably about as histori-cally accurate as *Operation: Burma*, the film that suggested that Errol Flynn liberated the Malay peninsula single-handedly. Rat Pack movies were less about how the world was than about how Sinatra saw it, and Frankie 'The Voice' saw the Pacific War as a great opportunity for hi-jinks and high drama. As much fun as the film is, *Never So Few* is only significant since it suggested to McQueen fans just how big their boy was going to be. Film 3/5, McQueen 3/5.

The Magnificent Seven (1960)

Cast: Yul Brynner (Chris), Horst Buchholz (Chico), Steve McQueen (Vin), Eli Wallach (Calvera), James Coburn (Britt), Charles Bronson (Bernardo O'Reilly), Robert Vaughn (Lee), Brad Dexter (Harry Luck), Vladimir Sokoloff (Old Man), Rosenda Monteros (Petra)

Crew: Director & Producer John Sturges, Writer William Roberts (screenplay adapted from *The Seven Samurai* by Akira Kurosawa, Shinobu Hashimoto & Hideo Oguni), Executive Producer Walter Mirisch, Associate Producer Lou Morheim, Music Elmer Bernstein, Cinematographer Charles Lang Jnr, Editor Ferris Webster, Costume Designer Bert Henrikson, 128 minutes

Story: Sick of having to give their harvest to bandit king Calvera, emissaries from a small Mexican village travel to the US to hire some help. There they meet the enigmatic Chris, a Cajun killer who sympathises with the Mexicans' cause. Despite little in the way of finances, Chris recruits a squad of gunmen - Harry Luck, who believes the Latinos are sitting on a pile of gold, knifeman Britt, the fun-lovin' Vin, muscle-bound Mexican-Irishman O'Reilly and gunslinger Lee who's on the run from the authorities. The six ride south for the border, accompanied by Chico, a young Mexican who is desperate to join the group. Once in the village, Chico proves his worth and is officially made a part of the seven. The band are suc-cessful in their first encounter with Calvera and proceed to teach the townsfolk how to defend themselves. In the final epic battle, Calvera and his cronies perish as do four of the seven; Harry still believing he is within touching distance of Eldorado, O'Reilly rescuing the children that have come to worship him, Lee having overcome the cowardice that has made him an outsider and Britt, whose reliance on an outmoded weapon finally catches up with him. Of the survivors, Chico has fallen in love with a local girl and decides to stay, leaving Chris and Vin to ride back to America in search of fresh adventure...

McQueen Off-Screen: Steve wasn't involved in the legal wrangling that threatened to overwhelm *The Magnificent Seven* (law suits were threatened by Anthony Quinn, who claimed Kurosawa had sold him the screenplay rights, The Screen Actors' Guild, rival studios - all sorts of people). He did, though, have something of a falling out with Yul Brynner when the bald one realised that Steve, rather than himself, had been cast in the role made famous by Toshiro Mifune in Kurosawa's movie. Although the scriptwriters did beef up Brynner's role, McQueen's part retained the same memorable qualities as the one played by Mifune.

After the success of *The Magnificent Seven*, producers looked to convert other Akira Kurosawa pictures for American audiences. In Italy, 1961's *Yojimbo* was recrafted as *A Fistful Of Dollars* (1963, dir Sergio Leone) and *Django* (1966, dir Sergio Corbucci). In America, meanwhile, Kurosawa's *Rashomon* (1950) was remade as *The Outrage* (1964, dir Martin Ritt) while George Lucas built elements of *The Hidden Fortress* (1958) into the little seen *Star Wars* (1976).

McQueen On-Screen: And just how memorable is Vin, the happy-go-lucky gunman? Well, if you ever play the 'name *The Magnificent Seven*' game in the pub, you can guarantee that you won't be searching for McQueen's names (people usually fall down on Brad Dexter or Horst Buchholz). Charming and wisecracking, Vin might be a little too glib for his own good but you always look forward to him being on camera and you're relieved that he isn't one of the good guys that buys it.

McQueen Quotables: i) Vin: "After a while you can call bartenders and faro dealers by their first name." ii) Vin: "We deal in lead, friend." iii) Vin: "Reminds me of that fellow back home that fell off a ten-story building." Chris: "What about him?" Vin: "Well, as he was falling people on each floor kept hearing him say, 'So far, so good.' Tch... so far, so good!" iv) Chris: "It's like this fellow I knew in El Paso. One day, he just took all his clothes off and jumped in a mess of cactus. I asked him that same question, 'Why?'" Chris: "And?" Vin: "He said, 'It seemed like a good idea at the time.'"

McQueen's Confederates: Besides being reunited with Sturges, Relyea and Bronson, Steve met and became close friends with James Coburn and Robert Vaughn, both of whom he would work with again. *The Magnificent Seven* also gave him an opportunity to work with fellow Neighbourhood Playhouse alumni Eli Wallach (here apparently rehearsing for the part of Tuco in *The Good, The Bad & The Ugly* (1965, dir Sergio Leone)).

McQueen cash: $100,000 - Steve's first six-figure pay day.

Legacy: The Magnificent Seven was followed by *Return Of The Seven* (1966, dir Burt Kennedy), *Guns Of The Magnificent Seven* (1969, dir Paul Wendkos) and *The Magnificent Seven Ride* (1972, dir George McCowan). Of the original cast, Brynner returned for the first sequel but wisely steered clear of the others. Sturges' film was also imaginatively remade by producer Roger Corman as the sci-fi drama *Battle Beyond The Stars* (1980, dir Jimmy T Murakami) and lent its structure to the final episode of the first, not very funny, series of *Blackadder*.

The Verdict: It's as rare to meet people who don't like *The Magnificent Seven* as it is people who haven't seen it. Like so many classics, its brilliance exists in its moments: James Coburn's blade work, McQueen's wisecracking, the spectacular gun battles, Robert Vaughn losing his life but defeating fear - the list could go on for pages. And for those who think that the film tramples over the memory of Kurosawa's movie, check out the scene in which Coburn's knife thrower dies, then compare it to the death of the swordsman in *The Seven Samurai*. As Sturges is a clever, sensitive film-maker so his movie is the very best sort of homage. Film 5/5, McQueen 4/5.

The Big Time, Sort Of

After his winning turn in *The Magnificent Seven*, you'd have thought all Steve had to do was sit by the phone and wait for the offers to role in. Success in a supporting role was no indicator that McQueen could carry a motion picture on his own, however. Desperate to prove his star quality, Steve accepted the first leading role that came his way...

The Honeymoon Machine (1961)

Cast: Steve McQueen (Lieutenant Fergie Howard), Brigid Bazlen (Julie Fitch), Jim Hutton (Jason Eldrige), Paula Prentiss (Pam Dunstan), Dean Jagger (Admiral Fitch), Jack Weston (Signalman Burford Taylor), Jack Mullaney (Ensign Beau Gilliam), Marcel Hillaire (Casino Inspector)

Crew: Director Richard Thorpe, Writer George Wells, Novel *The Golden Fleecing* Lorenzo Semple, Producer Lawrence Weingarten, Music Leigh Harline, Cinematographer Joseph LaShelle, Editor Ben Lewis, Art Directors George W Davis & Preston Ames, Costume Designer Helen Rose, 87 minutes

Story: Here's the proof that there were a lot of drugs being taken in the 60s. Poker night on the USS El Mira is interrupted by the announcement that Operation Honeymoon has been a success thanks to Max, a super computer able to pinpoint where and when a missile will land. Drinking in this information, Lieutenant Fergie Howard asks naval scientist Jason Eldrige whether Max would be able to tell where the ball on the roulette wheel will land. When he hears that the answer is 'yes,' Fergie promises to make his next shore leave a profitable one. He checks into an expensive hotel with his shipmates, Jason and Beau, and then hits the Venice Casino. The three soon find out that becoming rich won't be as easy as they think for the ship's Admiral is staying two floors above them in the same hotel! Should he find out what is happening... Who knows, or cares, what might happen!?

McQueen Off-Screen: Before Steve was offered the lead, the script for *The Honeymoon Machine* had been sent to Cary Grant.

McQueen On-Screen: Although he could play humorous as well as anyone (he delivers his zingers in *The Magnificent Seven* and

The Great Escape perfectly), Steve couldn't play comedy to save his life. Rather like Richard Dreyfuss, Jerry Lewis and the early Jim Carrey, he is one of those actors who thinks the secret to getting laughs is mugging and mannered delivery. As painful as his performance is, it should be noted that *The Honeymoon Machine* features one thing that appears in every Steve McQueen movie - a shot of the actor topless.

McQueen's Confederates: No McQueen regulars, here - just fading Oscar winner Dean Jagger and Jim Hutton, who would later co-star in Sam Peckinpah's *Major Dundee*. Steve did, however briefly, hook up with one of the extras, a beautiful young actress called Sharon Tate.

McQueen's Cash: $100,000, which wasn't bad for an actor in his first leading role with only one hit behind him.

The Verdict: *The Honeymoon Machine* was the only film Steve McQueen hated more than *The Blob*. Enough said? Film 1/5, McQueen 1/5.

Hell Is For Heroes (1962)

Cast: Steve McQueen (Private Reese), Bobby Darin (Private J J Corby), Fess Parker (Sergeant Parker), Nick Adams (Homer), Bob Newhart (Private James E Driscoll), Harry Guardino (Sergeant Larkin), James Coburn (Corporal Henshaw), Mike Kellin (Private Kolinski), Joseph Hoover (Captain Loomis), Bill Mullikin (Private Cumberly), L Q Jones (Sergeant Frazer), Michele Montau (Monique), Don Haggerty (Captain Mace)

Crew: Director Don Siegel, Writers Robert Pirosh & Richard Carr, Story Robert Pirosh, Producer Henry Blanke, Music Leonard Rosenman, Cinematographer Howard Lipstein, Editor Howard Smith, Art Directors Hal Pereira & Howard Richmond, Technical Advisor Major William H Harrigan, 90 minutes

Story: Demoted Sergeant Reese joins an army squadron led by his former colleague Sergeant Parker. Conscious that the Germans could break through the allied lines at any time, Parker scouts out the area leaving Sergeant Larkin in charge. While Parker is away, the small platoon make as much noise as possible to give the Jerries the impression that they are a full company of men. When Larkin is killed by the advancing Germans, Corporal Henshaw takes charge. Asking the disgraced Reese for his advice, Henshaw is told that if the troop are to have any chance of survival, they must seize the

German pillbox that lies across a minefield and controls the section opposite them. During their treacherous trek through the mines, Henshaw buys it. When Parker rejoins the group, he demands to know whose idea it was to attack the pillbox. Reese, now close to cracking, admits that the plan was his. He redeems himself by grabbing hold of a package of dynamite and diving into the pillbox, destroying it completely. Despite his sacrifice, the bloodshed and the killing continues...

McQueen Off-Screen: *Hell Is For Heroes* started out with co-writer Robert Pirosh in the director's chair but he quit a week into filming following rows with McQueen and Paramount head of production Marty Rackin. In his excellent autobiography *A Siegel Film*, substitute director Don Siegel recalls his first encounter with McQueen. "He explained how he worked with a director. He hoped I didn't mind if he looked through the camera on every shot. Me: 'I don't mind. The cameraman might though.' McQueen: (with modesty) 'Now, I throw ideas at the director all the time. Maybe four or five hundred. I don't say they're all good. Maybe only one hundred and fifty are useable.' Me: (breaking in) 'I don't care who I get the ideas from - the grip, the electrician. My name goes on the screen as director. But there's one thing you better be damn sure you understand (hitting the desk hard so everything bounces about) - I'm the director! Come hell or high water!'" Steve responded by threatening to punch Siegel out. It's remarkable that after such a fiery beginning, the pair weren't only able to complete the movie but actually got along quite well.

Thanks to *Wanted: Dead Or Alive* (which had come off air the previous year) and *The Magnificent Seven*, Steve possessed such star power that he was even able to get the title of Siegel's picture changed. Written as *Separation Hill*, the film was set to be released as *The War Story*. McQueen, who hated both monikers, suggested calling the picture *Hell Is For Heroes*, only to learn that that was the title of an Edmond O'Brien (*DOA*) picture that had just gone into production. Since Steve's star was on the rise and O'Brien's was on the wane, the young buck got what he wanted. O'Brien's film would eventually be released as *Man Trap*.

When *Hell Is For Heroes* first played in theatres, it was proceeded by a spoken introduction. The narrator was President John F Kennedy.

McQueen On-Screen: Reese gave McQueen the opportunity to show that there was more to him as an actor than the glibness that had made *The Magnificent Seven*'s Vin so attractive. The performance he gives here is occasionally a little fraught, but it proves that his range extended beyond one-liners. Indeed, Stanley Kubrick (who knew a thing or two about war movies) went so far as to describe Steve's turn as; "the best portrayal of a solitary soldier I've ever seen."

McQueen's Confederates: Fellow *Magnificent Seven* posse member James Coburn plays a corporal who shows how you can make a jeep sound like a tank. Also featured amongst the supporting cast are American comedian Bob Newhart, singer Bobby Darrin (ask your dad) and Peckinpah foot soldier L Q Jones.

McQueen Quotables: Larkin (referring to the decision to advance): "Were you right?" Reese: "How do I know?"

McQueen's Cash: $150,000.

Legacy: If you have not yet caught the excellent *Rushmore* (1998, dir Wes Anderson), then the fact that it contains a reference to *Hell Is For Heroes* provides the ideal excuse to rent it.

The Verdict: Sentimentalists have often said how sad it was that Don and Steve never hooked up again (Siegel was scheduled to direct *Tom Horn* but the deal fell through). Instead of moping over what never was, we should content ourselves with the great war movie Siegel created and the fine performance McQueen delivered. Film 4/5, McQueen 4/5.

The War Lover (1962)

Cast: Steve McQueen (Captain Buzz Rickson), Robert Wagner (Lieutenant Ed Bolland), Shirley Ann Field (Daphne Caldwell), Gary Cockrell (Gary Lynch), Michael Crawford (Junior Sailen), Billy Edwards (Brindt), Chuck Julian (Lamb), Robert Easton (Handown), Al Waxman (Prien), Tom Busby (Farr), George Sperdakos (Bragliani), Bob Kanter (Haverstraw), Jerry Stovin (Emmet), Edward Bishop (Vogt), Richard Leech (Murika), Bernard Braden (Randall), Sean Kelly (Woodman),

Charles De Temple (Braddock), Neil McCallum (Sully), Viera (Singer), Justine Lord (Street Girl), Louise Dunn (Hazel), Arthur Hewlett (Vicar)

Crew: Director Philip Leacock, Writer Howard Koch, Novel John Hersey, Producer Arthur Hornblow Jnr, Music Richard Addinsell, Cinematographer Bob Huke, Aerial Photographers Ron Taylor & Skeets Kelly, Editor Gordon Hales, Art Director Bill Andrews, Production Manager Robert Sterne, Costume Designer Elsa Fennell, Technical Advisors Lieutenant Colonel Robert F Spence & Lieutenant Colonel William Tesla, 105 minutes

Story: Buzz Rickson and Ed Bolland are American bomber pilots stationed in England during World War II. Rickson is a great pilot whose seat-of-the-pants flying upsets his superiors. Bolland, meanwhile, is a sensitive sort who hates killing but accepts that it is a part of his job. The pair become involved with a local girl, Daphne Caldwell. Although she is drawn to Rickson, she realises that it is only a physical attraction. Bolland, however, offers her genuine love and it is with the more introspective pilot that Daphne stays. When their plane is crippled over the English Channel, Bolland urges Rickson to bail out but he refuses. While Bolland jumps to safety, Rickson fails to land the aircraft and crashes into the white cliffs of Dover.

McQueen Off-Screen: Kicked out of the Savoy for setting fire to the curtains, McQueen divided his off-set time between a palatial Knightsbridge flat and Brands Hatch. Terrified that their star might get killed mid-shoot, Columbia inserted a clause into Steve's contract that said that should he die, he would be liable to pay the full cost of the picture ($2.3 million). He didn't race again until *The War Lover* wrapped.

By the way, if the name of author John Hersey sounds familiar that's because he also wrote the highly acclaimed *A Bell For Adano*, which was filmed in 1945 by Henry King and was discussed by Jack Nicholson and Art Garfunkel's characters in Mike Nichols' *Carnal Knowledge* (1971).

McQueen On-Screen: So often a grade-A asshole off-camera, it perhaps shouldn't be any surprise that McQueen is so good at playing the scoundrel on-screen. A wild for kicks, love 'em and leave 'em type, Rickson sees Steve using all his favourite tools (that famous smile is seldom far from his lips), although here, he brilliantly undercuts them with an air of arch-arrogance. The quality of his performance is even more impressive when you consider that he has little to work with (his co-stars include the wooden Shirley Anne Field and the man who would become Frank Spencer) and he has to cope with some appalling, pseudo-macho dialogue (see *McQueen Quotables*).

McQueen's Confederates: When Steve McQueen and Robert Wagner first met, they couldn't stand the sight of each other. After a couple of weeks of sparring, the pair became inseparable and promised to work together again which they did, eleven years later, in *The Towering Inferno*.

McQueen Quotables: i) Rickson: "Rules are for sergeants." ii) Rickson: "When you come up with a bomb big enough to blow up Rickson, you can blow up the world!"

McQueen's Cash: $75,000.

The Verdict: An excellent, if uncharacteristic, turn from McQueen is wasted on a dreadful dollop of wartime melodrama. Fortunately for Steve, a much better WWII was just around the corner. Film 2/5, McQueen 4/5.

The Great Escape (1963)

Cast: Steve McQueen (Captain Virgil Hilts, 'The Cooler King'), James Garner (Bob Hendley, 'The Scrounger'), Richard Attenborough (Squadron Leader Roger Bartlett, 'Big X'), James Donald (Ramsey, 'The SBO'), Charles Bronson (Danny Velinski, 'Tunnel King'), Donald Pleasence (Colin Blythe, 'The Forger'), James Coburn (Louis Sedgwick, 'The Manufacturer'), John Leyton (Willie, 'Tunnel King'), Gordon Jackson (Flight Lieutenant MacDonald, 'Intelligence'), David McCallum (Eric Ashley-Pitt, 'Disposal'), Nigel Stock (Cavendish, 'The Surveyor'), William Russell (Soren), Angus Lennie (Ives, 'The Mole'), Hannes Messemer (Von Luger, 'The Kommandant'), Robert Graf (Werner, 'The Ferret'), Tom Adams (Nimmo), George Mikell (Dietrich), Karl Otto Alberty (Steinach), Jud Taylor (Goff), Hans Reiser (Kuhn), Harry Riebauer (Strachwitz), Robert Freitag (Posen), Ulrich Beiger (Preissen), Lawrence Montaigne (Haynes), Robert Desmond (Griffith), Til Kiwe (Frick)

Crew: Director & Producer John Sturges, Writers James Clavell & W R Burnett, Associate Producer Robert Relyea, Music Elmer Bernstein, Cinematographer Daniel L Fapp, Editor Ferris Webster, Costume Designer Bert Henrikson, Technical Advisor C Wallace Floody MBE, 168 minutes

Story: You're probably as familiar with the plot of *The Great Escape* as you are with your date of birth. But if you're one of the two people who hasn't seen Sturges' ace movie, here's the briefest of recaps - It's 1943 and a band of allied officers plan an audacious escape from Stalag 17. Led by Roger 'Big X' Bartlett, the assorted Brits, Yanks and Aussies commence work on a complex operation involving three tunnels ('Tom,' 'Dick' and 'Harry') that they hope will result in the escape of 250 personnel. Besides Bartlett, the potential escapees include the charming but callow scrounger Hendley, claustrophobic Polish-born tunnel king Danny Velinski, the skilled but myopic forger Colin Blythe, British top brass 'Mac' MacDonald, Australian engineer Louie Sedgwick, the stuffy surveyor and choir master Cavendish and, last but by no means least, the ice cool king of solitary confinement, Virgil Hilts. The entire camp is set to work: printing visas and passes, making civilian clothes, hoarding supplies, drawing maps. The Nazis accidentally discover 'Tom,' but they never locate the other tunnels. When the night of the escape arrives, the allies discover that their tunnel is twenty feet too short. Rather than calling the evacuation off, Bartlett and Co. press on and by the time the Jerries uncover the operation, seventy five POWs have fled into the night. Of these, Bartlett, MacDonald and Cavendish are caught by the Germans and executed. Others like Blythe are shot during the act of escaping, while Hendley and Hilts - the latter of whom leads the Krauts a merry dance on his motorbike - are returned to the Stalag. Of the seventy-five escapees, only Aussie Louie Sedgwick and tunnel kings Danny and Willey make it to safety. The film is dedicated to the fifty men executed by the Nazis.

McQueen Off-Screen: According to James Coburn, McQueen was almost impossible to be around on the set of *The Great Escape*. "He kept saying: 'why can't these movies just be about one guy and why can't that guy be me?'" McQueen kicked up such a fuss that the studio flew out screenwriter W R Burnett who rewrote Virgil Hilts to Steve's specifications. It was a measure Coburn didn't fully approve of. "I don't think his character fits into the picture, wearing those jeans and that sweatshirt. And as for that baseball mit, well, Steve was the most unathletic guy in the world. If you threw a ball at him, he'd run away from it."

Legacy: The utterly superfluous *The Great Escape II - The Untold Story* starring Christopher Reeve, Donald Pleasance and

TV's *Lovejoy* Ian McShane was made for television in 1988. The original film is clearly a big favourite of the Zucker brothers and Jim Abrahams who sent up the dirt-down-the-trousers bit in *The Naked Gun 33 1/3* (1994) and recreated the bike chase shot-for-shot in *Top Secret* (1984). *The Great Escape* also provides the model for Nick Park's debut feature, *Chicken Run* (2000). As for Steve's great moments in the movie, the interview with Big X and Mac was doctored for an advert promoting Holsten Pils while his baseball antics were quite superbly spoofed by Maggie Simpson in the episode 'A Streetcar Named Marge.' Elmer Bernstein's stirring theme music, meanwhile, was the unofficial anthem of England's 1998 World Cup campaign.

McQueen On-Screen: Okay, so he doesn't look like a proper WWII soldier and he didn't perform the famous fence stunt. Aside from these small quibbles, McQueen's performance is faultless. Humorous, hard-as-nails, compassionate (the scene where he mourns the death of the doomed Angus Lennie): this is Steve doing all the things he does best. You can look long and hard but you won't find a better performance in an action movie. And don't just take my word for it - McQueen won the Best Actor award at the Moscow International Film Festival for his performance. Yes, that's right - at the height of the Cold War (the Cuban Missile Crisis occurred in 1962) the Ruskies gave their top acting gong to an All-American boy. If that's not a sign of a terrific turn, I don't know what is.

McQueen Quotables: i) Von Luger: "Hilts, isn't it?" Hilts: "Captain Hilts, actually." Von Luger: "Seventeen escape attempts." Hilts: "Eighteen." Von Luger: "Tunnel man, engineer?" Hilts: "Flier." Von Luger: "I suppose you're called in the American Army a 'hotshot pilot.'" Hilts: "Mmhmm." Von Luger: "Unfortunately, you were shot down anyway. So we are both grounded for the duration of the war." Hilts: "Well, you speak for yourself, Colonel." Von Luger: "You have other plans?" Hilts: "I haven't seen Berlin yet, from the ground or from the air, and I plan on seeing both before the war is over." Von Luger: "Are all American officers so ill-mannered?" Hilts: "About 99 percent." Von Luger: "Then perhaps while you are with us, you'll have a chance to learn something. Ten days isolation, Hilts." Hilts: "Captain Hilts." ii) Bartlett: "My name is Roger." Hilts: "Alright, Roger." Bartlett: "Yours is Virgil, isn't it?" Hilts: "Hilts. Just make it Hilts." iii) Hilts: "Something's coming. I can feel it and it's coming right around the corner at me, Squadron Leader!"

McQueen's Confederates: The Great Escape was Steve's third movie with John Sturges, Robert Relyea and James Coburn and his second with Charles Bronson. The film also marked the beginning of a brief professional association and lifelong friendship with Richard Attenborough. And as everyone should know by now, McQueen's motorcycle stunts were performed by Steve's old chum, world-champion bike rider Bud Ekins.

McQueen's Cash: $400,000, which wasn't at all bad considering that his previous movie had died on its ass.

The Verdict: The same thing happens in households across Britain every Boxing Day. You turn on the telly and there's *The Great Escape*. "Jesus Christ!" you bellow, "I don't pay my license fee to watch this every year." And then you sit down and you start to watch. You get caught up in the procedures of the escape. You get concerned about Charles Bronson's claustrophobia. You start to chuckle at James Coburn, who clearly knows that Australia has an accent but hasn't bothered to find out what it sounds like. Then, nearly three hours later, there you are getting all upset about the demise of Donald Pleasance and praying that Gordon Jackson will say 'merci' this time round. Somewhere there is a place where all action movies are like *The Great Escape*, all action movie performances are as excellent as McQueen's, Attenborough's and Garner's, and all action movie characters have nicknames in quotation marks like 'The Scrounger.' And if, when you reach the hereafter, you discover the cinemas aren't screening Sturges' movies, then you'll know you're in Hell. Film 5/5, McQueen 5/5.

A Star Is Born

After *The Great Escape*, McQueen had the fame to match his millions. He was now in a situation where he could make any picture he wanted. Rather than cementing his image as a star of action cinema, Steve decided to return to a genre which he had so far failed to master, comedy.

Soldier In The Rain (1963)

Cast: Jackie Gleason (Master Sergeant Maxwell Slaughter), Steve McQueen (Supply Sergeant Eustis Clay), Tuesday Weld (Bobby Jo Pepperdine), Tony Bill (Jerry Meltzer), Tom Poston (Lieutenant Magee), Ed Nelson (Military Police Sergeant Priest), Lew Gallo (Military Police Sergeant Lenahan), Paul Hartman (Chief Of Police), Chris Noel (Frances McCoy), Adam West (Captain Blekely)

Crew: Director Ralph Nelson, Writers Maurice Richlin & Blake Edwards, Novel William Goldman, Producers Martin Jurow & Blake Edwards, Music Henry Mancini, Cinematographer Philip Lathrop, Editor Ralph Winters, Art Director Phil Barber, Costume Designers Jerry Alpert & Shirlee Strahm, 87 minutes

Story: Supply Sergeant Eustis Clay has grown tired of life in the US military and tries to persuade his friend Sergeant Maxwell Slaughter to quit and start a business with him. Slaughter loves the army life but follows his friend with whom he get into all sorts of scrapes and seductions. Hospitalised after a brawl, Slaughter confesses to Clay that he longs to retire to a Pacific isle. It is a short-lived dream, however, as Slaughter passes away. Alone in the world, Clay decides to re-enlist. On his return to active service, he raises a glass to his fallen friend.

McQueen Off-Screen: It's easy to see why Steve decided that Solar Productions should make *Soldier In The Rain* its first picture. Adapted from a novel by William Goldman (who'd later strike it rich with the screenplays for *Butch Cassidy And The Sundance Kid* and *All The President's Men*), the film boasted the talents of director Ralph Nelson (*Lilies Of The Field*), screenwriter Blake Edwards (the brains behind *Breakfast At Tiffany's*, *The Days Of Wine And Roses* and *The Pink Panther*) and top comic actor Jackie Gleason (star of American TV classic *The Honeymooners*). All of these pluses should, however, have been overridden by the fact that STEVE McQUEEN COULDN'T PLAY COMEDY!

43

Owing to a remarkably insensitive piece of marketing, *Soldier In The Rain* opened on 27 November 1963, just five days after the assassination of President Kennedy.

McQueen On-Screen: Remember Kenneth Branagh trying to play horror in *Mary Shelley's Frankenstein*? Or John Malkovich's Muscovite card-sharp in John Dahl's *Rounders*? Or Jack Palance playing Castro in *Che*? Or Claude Raine's lip-smacking turn as Professor Challenger in *The Lost World*. Well, none of them are anywhere near as embarrassing as watching Steve McQueen play it for laughs. Get the children inside, mother, there's no need for them to see this.

McQueen's Confederates: McQueen considered Tuesday Weld one of the best actresses he'd ever worked with and insisted that, after Sam Peckinpah turned down Sharon Tate for the female lead in *The Cincinnati Kid*, the role be given to his *Soldier In The Rain* co-star. And 'holy squirrels in a cage, Batman!' Isn't that the young Adam West playing Captain Blekely?

McQueen Quotables: i) Slaughter: "I'm a narcissist." Clay: "I thought you were as crazy about girls as everybody." ii) Clay: "I rate women the way school teachers mark tests: A, B, C, D, F and incomplete."

McQueen's Cash: $300,000, which I imagine Steve banked with a decidedly sheepish grin on his face.

The Verdict: After watching *Soldier In The Rain*, sleep, wake up and pretend it was just a bad dream. Film 1/5, McQueen 1/5.

Love With The Proper Stranger (1963)

Cast: Natalie Wood (Angela Rossini), Steve McQueen (Rocky Papasano), Edie Adams (Barbara 'Barb' Margolis aka Barbara of Seville), Herschel Bernardi (Dominick Rossini), Tom Bosley (Anthony Columbo), Harvey Lembeck (Julio), Penny Santon (Mama Rossini), Arlene Golonka (Marge), Virginia Vincent (Anna), Nick Alexander (Guido Rossini), Augusta Ciolli (Mrs Papasano), Anne Hegira (Beetie), Mario Badolati (Elio Papasano), Elena Karam (Woman Doctor), Nina Varela (Mrs Columbo), Marilyn Chris (Gina), Wolfe Barzell (Priest), Keith Worthey (Negro Boy, uncredited), Henry Howard (Lou), Frank Marth (Carlos), Richard Bowler (Flower Vendor), Lennie Bremen (Truck Driver), Nobu McCarthy (Yuki), Jean Schulman (Charlene, uncredited), Lou Herbert (Harold), Barney Martin (Sidney), Michael Enserro (Moish, uncredited), Louis Guss (Flooey, uncredited), Tony Mordente (Fat, uncredited), Val Avery (Stein), Richard Mulligan (Louie, uncredited),

Paul Price (Klepp), Lorraine Abate (Maria, uncredited), Vincent Deadrick (Call Boy, uncredited), Richard A Dysart (Accountant, uncredited), Vic Tayback (Cye), Barney Steven (Sidney, uncredited)

Crew: Director Robert Mulligan, Writer Arnold Schulman, Producer Alan J Pakula, Music Elmer Bernstein, Cinematographer Milton Krasner, Editor Aaron Stell, Art Directors Hal Pereira & Roland Anderson, Production Manager Frank Caffey, Costume Designer Edith Head, 100 minutes

Story: Musician Rocky Papasano is paged at his Manhattan union hall by Angie, a department store worker with whom he had a brief fling. Angie tells Rocky that she is pregnant and asks him if he can recommend a doctor to perform an abortion. Not sure what to do, Rocky talks to his current girlfriend, a stripper called Barbie, who throws him out in a fit of jealousy. Unaware that she is pregnant, Angie's family try to set her up with Tony Columbo, a shy Italian restaurant owner who has proposed to her. Having found a doctor willing to help, Rocky tries to raise the money to pay for the operation. He also takes Angie to meet his parents who take to her immediately. Come the time of the abortion, Rocky refuses to let Angie go through with it. Although she loves him, Angie knows Rocky will never marry her, so she reconsiders Columbo's proposal since the restaurateur has told people that it is his baby Angie is carrying. Still unsure what to do, Angie tries to patch things up with Rocky but their conversation disintegrates into a bitter quarrel. Just as it looks as if the couple have broken up for good, Angie leaves work to find Rocky outside holding a sign reading; 'Better Wed Than Dead.'

McQueen Off-Screen: Desperate as McQueen was to break away from war movies, comedy wasn't the way to do it. A more viable escape route was offered by Alan J Pakula and Robert Mulligan, the producer/director team behind the Academy Award-winning adaptation of Harper Lee's *To Kill A Mockingbird*. Thanks to the two films he made with Mulligan and Pakula, McQueen was able to add 'sex symbol' to his resume.

According to biographers, Natalie Wood flirted outrageously with Steve throughout shooting. In a rare display of self-discipline McQueen, aware that Wood was Robert Wagner's girlfriend, declined her advances.

McQueen On-Screen: While his Italian jazz musician isn't that much more convincing than his Jewish DA in *Never Love A Stranger*, McQueen makes it through the film without forgetting any of his lines and bumping into the scenery. Which isn't much of an acting achievement, I know but sometimes, when you're Steve McQueen, efficient is all you need to be.

McQueen's Confederates: Vic Tayback would become a regular McQueen collaborator. Tom Bosley, on the other hand, would become Mr Cunnigham in *Happy Days*.

McQueen's Cash: $300,000.

The Verdict: Well acted with high production values and an Elmer Bernstein score, *Love With The Proper Stranger* would be a lot easier to like were it not so obviously engineered to win awards (nominated for five Oscars, it came away with nothing). As a romantic leading man, on the other hand, Steve McQueen looks as comfortable as he did on the back of a horse or the seat of a motor-cycle. Film 3/5, McQueen 3/5.

Baby, The Rain Must Fall (1963)

Cast: Lee Remick (Georgette Price Thomas), Steve McQueen (Henry Thomas), Don Murray (Deputy Slim Murray), Paul Fix (Judge Ewing), Josephine Hutchinson (Mrs Ewing), Ruth White (Miss Clara), Charles Watts (Mr Tillman), Carol Veazie (Mrs Tillman), Estelle Hearnsley (Catherine), Kimberley Block (Margaret Rose Thomas), Zamah Cunnigham (Mrs T V Smith), George Dunn (Counterman)

Crew: Director Robert Mulligan, Writer Horton Foote, Play *The Travelling Lady* Horton Foote, Producer Alan J Pakula, Music Elmer Bernstein, Cinematographer Ernest Laszlo, Editor Aaron Stell, Art Director Roland Anderson, Technical Advisor Billy Strange, 93 minutes

Story: Released from prison on parole, Henry Thomas returns to the Texan town that is his home. A singer in a local band, Henry feels under pressure to give up the rock & roll lifestyle and go back to school. The incompatibility of his dreams of stardom with his responsibilities as a husband and father are brought home to Henry when his wife Georgette and young daughter come to live with him. If things weren't bad enough, Henry then gets involved in a knife fight which jeopardises his parole. Afraid as he is of responsibility and imprisonment, there is one thing that scares Henry more than anything else - an ageing spinster who has always held him in her thrall...

McQueen Off-Screen: What happened during the making of *Baby, The Rain Must Fall* was considerably less interesting than two events that took place before filming began. The first event involved Steve being stalked by Alfred Thomas Pucci, an incident that showed the star that fame wasn't all it was cracked up to be. The second concerned Steve having his face ripped off while racing trail bikes for the US national team in Berlin. The extensive injuries to McQueen's cheek and lip took twelve months to heal. Having seen how facial wounds had curtailed Montgomery Clift's career, McQueen must have been very relieved when the bandages were removed and he was still beautiful.

As for the film, *Baby, The Rain Must Fall* was released two years after it was made in 1965 and didn't make a penny. Disappointed, McQueen said goodbye to Mulligan and Pakula and went looking for a new challenge.

McQueen On-Screen: I'm sure the stunning Lee Remick could have coaxed sexual chemistry out of a dead mackerel, but when McQueen's on screen with the late, great star, the celluloid threatens to melt. The 33-year-old Steve also has no problem conjuring up the arrogance and insecurities of a man in his early twenties. The other point of note about Steve's performance is that he did all his own singing and guitar work. This resulted in a soundtrack that contained more overdubs than Queen's 'Bohemian Rhapsody.' At least we can all be grateful that he didn't go down the same path as William Shatner. And Don Johnson. And David Soul. And Bruce Willis. And Telly Savalas. And...

McQueen's Confederates: Pakula, Mulligan and fat old Paul Fix.

McQueen's Cash: $300,000.

The Verdict: While it's a pity that, in adapting *The Travelling Lady* for the big screen, the focus of attention shifted from Georgette to Thomas, *Baby, The Rain Must Fall* remains a substantial slice of Southern Gothic, complete with a marvellous 'mad woman in the attic' finale. Throw in McQueen's perfect playing and you have a film well worth rediscovering. Film 4/5, McQueen 4/5.

The Cincinnati Kid (1965)

Cast: Steve McQueen (Eric Stoner 'The Cincinnati Kid'), Edward G Robinson (Lancey Howard 'The Man'), Ann-Margret (Melba Nile), Karl Malden (Shooter), Tuesday Weld (Christian Rudd), Joan Blondell (Lady Fingers), Rip Torn (William Jefferson Slade), Jack Weston (Pig), Cab Calloway (Yeller), Jeff Corey (Hoban), Theo Marcuse (Felix), Dub Taylor (Card Dealer), Milton Selzer (Sokal), Karl Swenson (Mr Rudd), Emile Genest (Cajun), Ron Soble (Danny), Irene Tedrow (Mrs Rudd), Midge Ware (Mrs Slade), Andy Albin (Referee, uncredited), Mimi Dillard (Slade's Girl Friend, uncredited), Robert DoQui (Philly, uncredited), Claude Hall (Gambler, uncredited), Virginia Harrison (Employee, uncredited), Harry Hines, Burt Mustin, William Challee & Charles Wagenheim (Old Man, uncredited), Breena Howard (Cajun's Woman, uncredited), Sandy Kevin, John Hart, Howard Wendell & Bill Zuckert (Poker Player, uncredited), Barry O'Hara (Eddie, uncredited), Joyce Perry (Mrs Hoban, uncredited), Olan Soule (Desk Clerk, uncredited)

Crew: Director Norman Jewison, Writers Ring Lardner Jnr & Terry Southern, Novel Richard Jessup, Producer Martin Ransohoff, Associate Producer John Calley, Music Lalo Schifrin, Cinematographer Philip Lathrop, Editor Hal Ashby, Art Directors George W Davis & Edward Carfagno, Technical Advisor Jay Ose, 102 minutes

Story: Eric Stoner is known to all as The Cincinnati Kid, the hottest young poker player in New Orleans. He has it all: the girls, the money, the notoriety. All that stands between him and immortality is national champion Lancey Howard, aka The Man. When the two finally meet, Slade, a local businessman who has dropped a bunch at the tables to Howard, tries to have the deck stacked in the Kid's favour but the young gun insists on playing it straight. When the night is through, The Kid has lost the card game, his fortune, his reputation and the true love of his life, Christian. He is plain Eric Stoner, once again (at least, that's what happens to the Kid in the US version of the film. In Asian prints of the movie, Stoner loses the game and his name but lives happily ever after with his girl).

McQueen Off-Screen: Had everything gone to plan, *The Cincinnati Kid* would have starred Steve McQueen, Spencer Tracy and Sharon Tate, been directed by Sam Peckinpah and been shot in black and white. Tracy, however, refused to play second fiddle to Steve, Peckinpah preferred Tuesday Weld to Tate and the director himself received his marching orders when he insisted on shooting a nude scene. 'Bloody Sam' was replaced by Norman Jewison, a young director whose previous experience comprised a couple of throwaway comedies and whose sole artistic contribution to *The Cincinnati Kid* was his insistence that no primary colours be used(!). With such a young blood at the helm, it was left up to McQueen to supply the film's magic.

McQueen On-Screen: And supply it he did. Having no doubt seen the film for what it was - a thinly disguised remake of Paul Newman vehicle *The Hustler* (1961, dir Robert Rossen) - McQueen resists the obvious temptation to revive 'Fast' Eddie Felson and instead creates a unique, compelling character: a man who speaks little but says lots, who exudes confidence but lives in constant fear of defeat. And, along the way, Steve gives the audience all the things he knows they like: the smile, the shirt off, the fisticuffs (the fight in the toilet was written into the script at McQueen's insistence).

McQueen's Confederates: The first of four films Steve would make with the wonderful character actor Dub Taylor, *The Cincinnati Kid* also featured McQueen's *Soldier In The Rain* co-star Tuesday Weld and a score by Lalo (*Bullitt*) Schifrin. It being a Norman Jewison movie, the film also featured the editing skills of Hal Ashby (later the director of *The Last Detail* and *Harold And Maude*).

McQueen Quotables: Cincinnati Kid: "Listen, Christian, after the game, I'll be The Man. I'll be the best there is. People will come and sit down at the table with you, just so they can say they played with The Man. That's what I'm gonna be."

McQueen's Cash: $350,000. The cheques just keep on getting bigger and bigger.

The Verdict: There's a lot to like about *The Cincinnati Kid*. Edward G Robinson eats up the screen as Lancey Howard, Tuesday Weld and Ann-Margret are both drop-dead gorgeous and Karl Malden, Rip Torn and Dub Taylor are clearly having a ball. While the cast are all on top form, there's no escaping the fact that the script (rewritten more times than a nervous best man's speech) is barely adequate and, try as he might, Norman Jewison hasn't got Sam Peckinpah's knack of elevating an everyday story to mythic heights. Whatever feathers the film has, there are no flies on McQueen. Having spent the last three films looking for a marketable screen persona, here he found one that would make him a legend - 'The King Of Cool.' Film 3/5, McQueen 4/5.

Icon

The Cincinnati Kid proved two things about Steve McQueen: i) his presence on screen was truly compelling and ii) his presence in a picture guaranteed gigantic financial success. One of the biggest names in the business, in the two years that followed McQueen would make the jump from simple movie star to genuine screen icon.

Nevada Smith (1966)

Cast: Steve McQueen (Nevada Smith/Max Sand), Karl Malden (Tom Fitch), Brian Keith (Jonas Cord), Suzanne Pleshette (Pilar), Janet Margolin (Neesa), Arthur Kennedy (Bill Bowdre), Howard Da Silva (Warden), Raf Vallone (Father Zaccardi), Pat Hingle (Big Foot), Martin Landau (Jesse Coe), Paul Fix (Sheriff Bonell), Gene Evans (Sam Sand), Josephine Hutchinson (Elvira McCanles), John Doucette (Ben McCanles), Iron Eyes Cody (Taka-Ta), Edy Williams (Saloon Girl), Sheldon Allman (Sheriff), Lyle Bettger (Jack Rudabough), Bert Freed (Quince), David McLean (Romero), Steve Mitchell (Buckshot), Merritt Bohn (Riverboat Pilot), Sandy Kenyon (Bank Clerk), Ricardo Roman (Cipriano), Josh Lawrence (Hogg), Stanley Adams (Storekeeper), George Mitchell (Paymaster), John Litel (Doctor), Ted De Corsica (Hudson), Strother Martin (Barney), L Q Jones (Cowboy)

Crew: Director & Producer Henry Hathaway, Writer John Michael Hayes, Novel *The Carpetbaggers* by Howard Robbins, Music Alfred Newman, Cinematographer Lucien Ballard, Editor Frank Bracht, Art Directors Hal Pereira & Tambi Larsen & Al Roelofs, Production Manager Frank Caffey, Costume Designer Frank Beetson Jnr, Second Unit Director Richard Talmadge, Assistant Directors Daniel J McCauley & Jospeh Lenzi, 131 minutes

Story: When his parents are murdered by three bandits, half-breed Max Sand promises to avenge their deaths. Setting off on his quest, Sand is joined by gunsmith Jonas Cord who tries to convince the young gunman that his mission is suicidal. Seeing that Sand is sincere, Cord shows him how to defend himself. Searching town after town, Max eventually finds one of the killers, Jesse Coe, and kills him in a knife fight. Injured in the affray, Sand has his wounds healed by Neesa, a young Indian girl, before setting off for Louisiana where he has heard that another of the murderers is imprisoned. Sand stages a hold-up and is thrown in jail where he meets and befriends the killer, Bill Bowdre. The pair escape the prison, only for Sand to shoot the desperado. Five years have now passed since Sand began his quest. No longer a green cowhand, he is as hardened a criminal as the men he has been pursuing. When he tracks down the final gunslinger, Tom Fitch, Sand shoots him in both legs but is unable to kill him. Instead, he throws away his gun and visits Jonas Cord to ask him for a job. Now calling himself Nevada Smith, he hopes to make a new life for himself

McQueen Off-Screen: After the huge success of *The Carpetbaggers*, author Harold Robbins suggested to producer Ted Levine that he take one of the book's characters, the movie cowboy Nevada Smith, and make a film about his origins. Figuring that he already owned the property, Levine set screenwriter John Michael Hayes to work right away.

That Steve was remarkably subdued during the making of *Nevada Smith* might have had something to do with his first meeting with director Henry Hathaway. Hathaway was the Sam Peckinpah of his generation. A tyrannical figure who'd once ordered that a house be torn down since it was ruining a shot. Hathaway, having heard about Steve's tendency to ride directors to the rail, set out his stall during their first meeting. "Mr McQueen," he barked, "I want you to know something: I'm the boss. Nobody argues with me. I'm not putting up with any shit from you and if I do get any shit from you, I won't hesitate to deck you. I don't want any of this star complex bullshit." Steve didn't so much as complain about the air conditioning after that.

McQueen On-Screen: Steve had only one thing to do in *Nevada Smith*; convince the world that he was a man half his age. Such is the quality of McQueen's performance, you aren't for a single moment conscious that this boy in his late teens is being played by a 36-year-old. *Nevada Smith* also features a notable scene in which McQueen drapes his arms over a shotgun to form a crucifix, à la James Dean. You can only imagine that the scene made it into the movie because Steve wanted it included. But why Steve should have wanted to pay homage to Dean is hard to understand - not only was McQueen by far the bigger star but he was a much more naturalistic (read: believable) actor than the ticky, grandstanding Dean.

McQueen's Confederates: Having enjoyed Karl Malden's hammy turn in *The Cincinnati Kid*, McQueen insisted that he return for *Nevada Smith*. As for Martin Landau, the last time Steve had worked with the actor was while they were studying at the Actors' Studio. *Nevada Smith* also features stunt work from Steve's favourite double Loren Janes, who also happened to be Hathaway's daredevil of choice. Meanwhile, L Q Jones, Strother Martin, Paul Fix and cinematographer Lucien Ballard were fully paid-up members of Sam Peckinpah's screen company, although McQueen had previously worked with Jones on *Hell Is For Heroes* and with Fix on *Baby, The Rain Must Fall*.

McQueen's Cash: $500,000 plus a motorhome (which he was allowed to keep after the film wrapped) and a 24-hour-a-day cordon bleu chef (which he wasn't).

Legacy: A second *Carpetbaggers* spin-off picture, a Hollywood fable called *Rina Marlowe*, was mooted but never made. *Nevada Smith* was remade for TV in 1975, with Cliff Potts in the title role (no, I haven't heard of him, either).

Verdict: Not only is *Nevada Smith* artistically empty, but thanks to its being shot on dreadful EastmanColor stock, it is also unattractive to look at. The film's only redeeming feature is McQueen, who does everything that's asked of him. Crap as it was, the film made an absolute mint, catapulting Steve to new heights of fame. Film 2/5, McQueen 3/5.

The Sand Pebbles (1966)

Cast: Steve McQueen (Jake Holman), Richard Attenborough (Frenchy), Richard Crenna (Captain Collins), Candice Bergen (Shirley Eckert), Marayat Andriane [aka Emmanuelle Arsan] (Maily), Mako (Po-Han), Larry Gates (Mr Jameson), Charles Robinson (Ensign Bordelles), Simon Oakland (Stawski), Gavin McLeod (Crosley), Joseph di Reda (Shanahan), Ford Rainey (Harris), Joe Turkel (Bronson), Richard Loo (Major Chin), Barney Phillips (Franks), Gus Trikonis (Restorff), Shepherd Sanders (Perna), James Jeter (Farren), Tom Middleton (Jennings), Paul Chinpae (Cho-jen), Tommy Lee (Chien), Beulah Quo (Mama Chunk), James Hong (Victor Shu), Stephen Jahn (Haythorn), Stephen Ferry (Lamb), Ted Fish (CPO Wellbeck), Loren James (Coleman), Glenn R Wilder (Waldron), Alan Hopkins (Wilsey), Gil

Perkins (Customer, uncredited), Walter Reed (Bidder, uncredited), Henry Wang (Lop-eye Shing, uncredited), Ben Wright (Englishman, uncredited)

Crew: Director & Producer Robert Wise, Writer Richard Anderson, Novel Richard McKenna, Associate Producer Charles H Maguire, Music Jerry Goldsmith, Cinematographer Joseph MacDonald, Editor William Reynolds, Production Designer Boris Leven, Technical Advisor Harvey Misiner, 193 minutes

Story: 1926. As nationalist feelings engulf China, the US gunboat San Pablo patrols the Yangtze. The newest member of the 'Sand Pebbles' (the nickname for the San Pablo's crew) is machinist Jake Holman. A loner at heart, Jake, nevertheless, befriends Frenchy, a sailor in love with a Chinese girl, Maily, who has been sold into prostitution. With China on the brink of civil war, the San Pablo confines itself to protecting the American civilians in the region, including missionary Jameson and a teacher called Shirley. To try and provoke the San Pablo, the Chinese flay Jake's coolie, Po-han. Jake ends his friend's torture by shooting him. Frenchy, meanwhile, has bought Maily's freedom and they marry. Frenchy swims ashore each night to visit Maily but he catches pneumonia and dies. When Jake visits Maily, the Chinese beat him, kill Maily and frame Jake for the murder. While the crew agree that Jake should stand trial, the kindly Captain Collins refuses and takes the ship upstream, away from trouble. When word arrives that full-scale fighting has led to the landing of US Marines in Shanghai, Captain Collins decides to give his humiliated ship and disgraced crew a chance to redeem themselves by freeing Jameson's mission station. However, when the San Pablo arrives, Jameson and Shirley declare themselves stateless and harangue the captain for interfering in Chinese affairs. The Chinese storm the mission and kill Jameson and Collins. Having earlier considered desertion, Jake redeems himself in his own eyes by providing the escaping Shirley with cover fire. Overwhelmed by the advancing Chinese, Jake perishes. His final words: "I was home.... What the hell happened?"

McQueen Off-Screen: For neither the first (*Love With The Proper Stranger*) nor last (*The Thomas Crown Affair*) time in his career, Steve McQueen accepted a role that had originally been offered to Paul Newman. While he would have liked to have tapped Newman's star power, Robert Wise couldn't have been happier with McQueen's performance ("He was so real and so right").

Wise, who'd dashed off *The Sound Of Music* simply to get studio backing for *The Sand Pebbles*, had somewhat more to say about the movie's symbolic value: "I wanted to show that American military might have been unpopular for many years, that the phrase 'Yankee, Go Home!' wasn't just something that came along post-World War II, but that it had been in existence the whole century. *The Sand Pebbles* came along just at the time when we were starting to get into Vietnam. For me, the message of the film was to make that point, that Vietnam should be seen in historical context."

Guys without girlfriends will be interested to learn that, at $250,000, the USS San Pablo was the most expensive prop ever constructed.

McQueen On-Screen: In later life, McQueen would talk openly about how much he disliked his performance in *The Sand Pebbles*. His disgust probably stemmed from the fact that Jake Holman doesn't behave like your average McQueen character (he kills a colleague [albeit to put him out of pain], he contemplates desertion, he doesn't get the girl, he dies, etc.). The difficult nature of the shoot might also have soured his feelings towards Holman (Steve spent his free time cooped up in a one-room house in a Taiwanese paddy field with a wife and two small children). Although he has been better on screen (*The Great Escape*, *Bullitt*, *Junior Bonner*, *Tom Horn*), there is a desperation and incredible loneliness about Jake Holman that make him one of Steve's more memorable creations. You certainly wouldn't begrudge him his Golden Globe and Oscar nominations. And hats off, too, to McQueen for choosing to do a risky, political picture over the mindless but infinitely more box office-friendly Ted Levine comedy he'd also been offered, *The Ski Bum*.

McQueen's Confederates: No one was more chuffed to see Steve McQueen become a big star than Robert Wise, the man who first cast Steve in a motion picture. Richard Attenborough must also have been pleased that, after befriending McQueen on the set of *The Great Escape*, the young actor had built on his fame rather than blown it.

McQueen's Cash: $250,000 plus gross participation. Once the receipts were in, *The Sand Pebbles* would prove to be McQueen's biggest screen pay day yet ($500,000).

The Verdict: *The Sand Pebbles* belongs to that time when film producers, frightened by the popularity of television, were desperate to give audiences things they couldn't get at home. Hence the big names, the expensive production values and the long running time. Watching the film on video cassette today, two things strike you, i) the quality of McQueen's performance and ii) the fact that *The Sand Pebbles* is a good hour longer than it needs to be.
Film 2/5, McQueen 4/5.

The Thomas Crown Affair (1968)

Cast: Steve McQueen (Thomas Crown), Faye Dunaway (Vicky Anderson), Paul Burke (Eddy Malone), Jack Weston (Erwin Weaver), Yaphet Kotto (Carol), Biff McGuire (Sandy), Todd Martin (Benjy), Sam Melville (Dave), Addison Powell (Abe), Sidney Armus (Arnie), Jon Shank (Curley), Allen Emerson (Don), Harry Cooper (Ernie), Johnny Silver (Bert), Astrid Heeren (Gwen), Carol Corbett (Miss Sullivan), John Orchard (John), Gordon Pinsent (Jamie MacDonald), Patrick Horgan (Danny), Peg Shirley (Honey Weaver), Leonard Caron (Jimmy Weaver), Ted Gehring (Marvin), Nora Marlowe (Marcie), Judy Pace (Pretty Girl), Tom Rosqui (Private Detective), Michael Shillo (Swiss Banker), Nikita Knatz (Sketch Artist), Carole Kelly (Motel Girl), Charles Lampkin & James Rawley & Paul Verdier (Elevator Operators), Victor Creatore & Paul Rhone (Cash Room Guards), Richard Bull (Booth Guard), Patty Regan (Girl In Elevator)

Crew: Director & Producer Norman Jewison, Writer Alan R Trustman, Associate Producer & Editor Hal Ashby, Music Michel Legrand, Cinematographer Haskell Wexler, Multiple Screens & Titles Pablo Ferro Films, Art Director Robert Boyle, Production Designer Edward G Boyle, Costume Designers Theadora Van Runkle & Ron Postal, Production Manager James E Henderling, Assistant Directors Walter Hill & Jack Reddish, Technical Advisors Alfred Sheinwald & Gary Wooten, 102 minutes

Also Known As: The Crown Caper, Thomas Crown & Company

Story: Self-made man Thomas Crown orchestrates the elaborate robbery of his own Boston bank using five operatives who have never met one another and have never seen his face. Delighted with his well-executed caper, Crown deposits the proceeds from the theft in a Swiss bank account. Having reimbursed Crown's bank for its losses, the insurance company assigns its top operative, Vicky Anderson, to investigate the enigmatic millionaire. Teamed with police lieutenant Eddy Malone, Vicky is introduced to Crown and his world of expensive playthings (polo ponies, gliders). After seducing one another over a chessboard, the pair begin an affair. Vicky fails to convince Malone to accept the stolen money in exchange for Crown's freedom. Crown, meanwhile, tells his lover that he is planning another theft and arranges to meet her after the heist in a local cemetery. Vicky arrives at the rendezvous with a police escort. When Crown's Rolls Royce pulls up it contains not the multimillionaire but a boy bearing a telegram: "Left early... You bring the money - or keep the car." A tearful Vicky looks to the skies where a jet speeds Crown to freedom.

McQueen Off-Screen: "I can honestly say he's the most difficult actor I ever worked with," claimed director Norman Jewison of Steve McQueen, "but he has such power!" It was for this reason that, three years after the hellish *Cincinnati Kid* shoot, Jewison said 'what the heck' and signed on to direct McQueen in *The Thomas Crown Affair*.

By 1968, Steve was better qualified than most to play the man who had everything. A production deal with Warner Brothers guaranteed him $750,000 a picture plus 50% of the profits. As the head of Solar Pictures, meanwhile, his 61% stake earned him upwards of $500,000 per annum.

Asked by interviewers to explain Steve's appeal to women, Faye Dunaway replied: "he stimulates that cuddly feeling. He's the misunderstood bad guy you're sure you can cure with a little warmth and home cooking." As for Dunaway's smooch over the chess set with McQueen, at 55 seconds, it is the longest kiss in cinema history.

McQueen On-Screen: Steve doesn't really act in *The Thomas Crown Affair*, rather he spends the whole time doing the things he liked doing best: driving fast cars, flying his aircraft, getting off with beautiful women, etc. A fantasy role, the only thing Crown and McQueen didn't share was a sense of style. However, for a guy who claimed he hated wearing suits, Steve sports an Armani as well as he wears that smile.

McQueen's Confederates: Both the assistant directors on *The Thomas Crown Affair* would work with Steve again: Walter Hill as an AD on *Bullitt* and as the author of *The Getaway* screenplay, and Jack Reddish as a co-owner of Solar Pictures. Steve also struck up a working relationship with the film's costume designer, Theadora Van Runckle (his contract allowed him to keep his entire wardrobe).

McQueen's Cash: $700,000, plus all the Italian suits he could carry.

Legacy: *The Thomas Crown Affair* was remade in 1997 by John McTiernan (*Die Hard I & III*, *The Hunt For Red October*), starring Pierce Brosnan and Rene Russo. One of the few remakes to actually outstrip the original, the film featured a cameo from Faye Dunaway as Crown's psychiatrist.

While Jewison's film was gloriously sent up in the *Austin Powers* movies, clips from the picture appear in both *Being There* (1979, dir Hal Ashby) and the Sandra Bullock/Dennis Leary comedy *Stolen Hearts* (aka *Two If By Sea*, 1996, dir Bill Bennett).

The Verdict: *The Thomas Crown Affair* isn't so much like watching a movie as flicking through a fashion catalogue. But, while periodicals make for a piss poor diet, it's quite nice to leaf through a glossy once in a while. And, likewise, it's also occasionally great to see a film star, especially one as appealing as Steve McQueen, doing exactly what they bloody well like. Completely empty then, but highly entertaining. Film 3/5, McQueen 3/5.

Bullitt (1968)

Cast: Steve McQueen (Lieutenant Frank Bullitt), Robert Vaughn (Walter Chalmers), Jacqueline Bisset (Cathy), Don Gordon (Delgetti), Robert Duvall (Weissberg/Taxi Driver), Simon Oakland (Captain Sam Bennet), Norman Fell (Captain Baker), Carl Reindel (Carl Stanton), Felice Orlandi (Albert Edward Renick), Vic Tayback (Pete Ross), Robert Lipton (First Aide), Ed Peck (Wescott), Pat Renella (Johnny Ross), Paul Genge (Mike), John Aprea (Killer), Al Checo (Desk Clerk), Bill Hickman (Phill), George S Brown (Surgeon, uncredited), Barbara Bosson (Nurse, uncredited), Chuck Dorsett (Airport Counter Person, uncredited)

Crew: Director Peter Yates, Writers Alan R Trustman & Harry Kleiner, Novel *Mute Witness* Robert L Pike (aka Robert L Fish), Producer Philip D'Antoni, Associate Producer Robert E Relyea, Music Lalo Schifrin, Cinematographer William A Fraker, Editor Frank P Keller, Titles Pablo Ferro Films, Art Director Albert Brenner, Costume Designers Alan Levine & Theadora Van Runkle, 114 minutes

Story: Lieutenant Bullitt and his partner Detective Delgetti are assigned by Captain Bennet of the San Francisco Police department to guard a Mafia informant who is to appear at a Senate hearing. A gangland hit leaves Delgetti wounded and the stool pigeon at death's door. When the informant dies, Bullitt insists that he be treated as if he is still alive to give the police time to find the killer and the man who leaked the stooly's address. Enter Walter Chalmers, a politician who is less concerned with the deceased than with the court hearing that will elevate him to high estate. Chalmers is intent on shutting Bullitt's investigation down, but the lawman won't hear of it. After doing away with the informant's killers, the dogged detective vows to get to the bottom of the case...

Lieutenant Bullitt and his partner Detective Delgetti are assigned to guard Johnny Ross, a Mafia informant who is scheduled to appear at a Senate crime hearing. A gangland hit leaves Delgetti wounded and the stool pigeon at death's door. When Ross is then murdered in hospital, Bullitt insists that the informant is treated as if he is still alive, a cunning ruse that gives him time to track the killers (who he chases to their deaths) and enables him to escape the wrath of Walter Chalmers, an ambitious politician determined to use build his reputation on Ross's testimony. As he investigates the case further, Bullitt discovers that the dead man was merely a decoy for the real Ross. With the Mafioso set to fly to London that evening, Bullitt races to the airport where, after confronting the spineless Chalmers, he pursues Ross onto the runways...

McQueen On-Screen: There's been so much talk about *Bullitt*'s amazing car chase that people have completely overlooked a performance that is as impressive as any in the McQueen canon. Thwarted, dissatisfied, puzzled; this is a McQueen we hadn't seen on camera before. Indeed, the scope of the mess Bullitt gets himself into, together with Steve's sensitive playing, creates a very real feeling that McQueen's character might not come out of the situation unscathed. (This sense of unease is cleverly exaggerated by Yates who, by using low angles, is even able to make something as straightforward as the good lieutenant visiting a Mexican restaurant a cause for concern.) McQueen once said that the way he made

Bullitt distinct from other movie cops was by playing the part in a turtleneck; characteristic modesty from a man whose talents more than matched the extent of his stardom.

McQueen Off-Screen: Set up in 1961, Steve had used Solar Productions as a tax dodge rather than a means to making the sort of films he wanted (the company had sunk cash into *Soldier In The Rain*, *The Cincinnati Kid* and *The Thomas Crown Affair*). As Solar lurched towards financial ruin, McQueen and his partners, Robert Relyea & Jack Reddish, looked for a property that would not only save the company but make it a force to be reckoned with.

A film which paved the way for the modern, stunt-driven blockbuster, it's amazing to think that *Bullitt* very nearly didn't get made. Warners' execs had been unable to find anyone able to successfully adapt Robert L Pike's novel *Mute Witness* and were ready to write the project off when Solar showed an interest in the property. McQueen wasn't too impressed with the adaptations either but he saw within the scripts a story line upon which he could hang the mixture of violence, action and seduction his fans had come to expect.

To prepare for their roles, McQueen and Don Gordon spent a couple of days with the San Francisco Police Department. The cops weren't too impressed with McQueen and tried to spook him by inviting him on a tour of the morgue. Steve duly showed up carrying a packed lunch.

Bullitt's celebrated car chase took three weeks to shoot. McQueen started off performing all the stunts himself but a close shave and a long chat with his wife convinced him to leave the driving to close friend Bud Ekins. As excellent as the chase sequence is, keep an eye out for how many times Bullitt overtakes the green VW Beetle and, after the Charger explodes, see if you can't spot the exact same Dodge being driven in the background of the very next shot. Such errors are quite understandable when you consider that, having been told by Peter Yates to drive at between 75 and 80 mph, Ekins and fellow stuntman Carey Loftin proceeded to roar about at speeds in excess of 100 mph.

Interviewed about *Bullitt* in 1997, Don Gordon remembered a conversation he had with McQueen shortly before the film wrapped. "One night we were driving home from the airport. We'd been working all night and the sun was just coming up. Steve said; 'Whadda you think? You think this movie's gonna be good?' I said; 'It's gonna be better than good.' The penny had dropped with me back in the second week. Steve said; 'You're lying.' I said; 'I'll tell you what, I'll give Solar back my salary if you give me 10% of the gross.' He just stared and said; 'Go fuck yourself. I'm not doing that.' I said; 'You see, you believe me.'" Had he received the percentage he asked for, Gordon would have been able to retire from acting before the start of the 1970s. As it was, he continued to work as a supporting actor, appearing in pictures like *Lethal Weapon* (1987, dir Richard Donner) and *Exorcist III* (1991, dir William Peter Blatty), before quitting for good in 1995.

Asked about the film by *Neon* magazine, Peter Yates said: "People talk more about *Bullitt* than any other of my films. I've had two films nominated for an Academy Award (*Breaking Away* and *The Dresser*) and they still want to talk about that damned car chase."

McQueen's Confederates: All the usual suspects (Don Gordon, Robert Relyea, Jack Reddish, Robert Vaughn and, uncredited, Walter Hill), plus composer Lalo Schifrin, whom McQueen hired having liked his contribution to *The Cincinnati Kid*, and character actor and Steve's drinking buddy Vic Tayback.

McQueen Quotes: Bullitt: "Look, you work your side of the street and I'll work mine."

McQueen's Cash: A cool \$1 million. Despite his huge pay cheque, McQueen demanded that the studio meet his standard rider requirements - ten pairs of jeans and ten electric razors. Only after his death was it revealed that Steve donated these items to Boys Republic, the correction centre he'd been sent to as a teen.

Legacy: Every few years, some smart young director comes along and tries to outdo *Bullitt*'s stunt extravaganza. Some, like William Friedkin (*The French Connection*, *To Live & Die In LA*), get very close. In the end, however, they're all left in the wake of McQueen's speeding Mustang.

Brilliantly spoofed in Sam Raimi's *Evil Dead II: Dead By Dawn*, *Bullitt* is homaged in Michael Mann's *Heat* (the thrilling airport finale), Tony Scott's *True Romance* and Hal Needham's *Hooper*. A clip from the Yates' film also appears in Stuart Baird's *Fugitive* sequel, *US Marshals*. *Bullitt* also inspired the superb stunt sequence in *Good Time Slim, Uncle Doobie & The Great Frisco Freak-out*, a vehicle for Troy McClure, who some of you might remember from such movies as *Calling All Quakers* and *The Revenge Of Abe Lincoln*.

The Verdict: What's there to say other than that *Bullitt* is one of the best cop movies ever and McQueen's performance rivals any in the genre. Film 5/5, McQueen 5/5.

The Reivers (1969)

Cast: Steve McQueen (Boon Hogganbeck), Sharon Farrell (Corrie), Will Geer (Boss), Rupert Crosse (Ned McCaslin), Mitch Vogel (Lucius McCaslin), Burgess Meredith (Narrator), Clifton James (Sheriff Butch Lovemaiden), Juano Hernandez (Uncle Possum), Dub Taylor (Dr Peabody), Allyn Ann McLerie (Alison McCaslin), Diana Shalet (Hannah), Diane Ladd (Phoebe), Ellen Geer (Sally)
Crew: Director Mark Rydell, Writers Irving Ravetch & Harriet Frank Jnr, Novel William Faulkner, Producer Irving Ravetch, Executive Producer Robert Relyea, Music John Williams, Cinematographer Richard Moore, Editor Thomas Stanford, Art Director Charles Bailey, Costume Designer Theadora Van Runkle, 111 minutes

Also Known As: Yellow Winton Flyer

Story: The Deep South, the early 1900s and a disparate group of folk travel to Memphis, Tennessee, in their Yellow Winton Flyer automobile. The travellers comprise slack-jawed goof-off Boon, young lad Lucius, negro Ned and whore-with-a-heart Corrie. Highlights of the journey include the motor car getting caught in a bog and eleven-year-old Lucius winning a horse race. There are a few laughs, a lot of mud and then the credits roll. Would you like your money back?

McQueen Off-Screen: After the staggering box office success of *Bullitt*, Steve could have made any picture he wanted. Dozens of projects were talked about: *Suddenly Single*, *Applegate's Gold*, *Swap*. Instead of making another event movie, Steve hooked up with Cinema Center and returned to something he hadn't done since the early 60s, comedy.

The Reivers could have been an intimate, charming study of days long gone. That it wasn't had everything to do with the involvement of Steve McQueen. With Steve attached, any notion of the picture being small disappeared. The focus of the film also shifted because of McQueen. In the book, young Lucius is our hero, but in the film Boon Hogganbeck becomes the film's centre of attention simply because he was played by the biggest actor in the world. Besides upsetting the film's conceit, Steve upset the balance of the cast list, too. Throw a huge star in amongst a bunch of character actors, even really good ones like Rupert Crosse, Clifton James and Dub Taylor, and a picture begins to look decidedly top heavy.

McQueen didn't do much for the on-set atmosphere, either. Remembers Mark Rydell: "He was hard and he could be mean and he did have me with my back to the wall sometimes. He wanted to feel that nothing could happen without him. He was an entirely instinctive actor. He never learned his lines and after one, or at the most, two takes, he wasn't any good." Like Norman Jewison, Rydell never hesitated in saying that McQueen was the most difficult actor he'd worked with.

In between set-ups, Steve spent most of his time training with his martial arts tutor Bruce Lee.

McQueen On-Screen: As man-child Boon Hogganbeck, McQueen delivers a performance so hammy, you could buy slices of it at your local delicatessen. You'd have thought that after *The Honeymoon Machine* and *Soldier In The Rain*, he would have learnt that he wasn't best suited to humour. As it was, it wasn't until after reflecting on his work in *The Reivers*, that McQueen decided never to do out-and-out comedy again.

McQueen's Confederates: Besides Dub Taylor and Theadora Van Runkle, director Mark Rydell had been a friend of McQueen's ever since introducing Steve to Neile in 1955 (Steve returned the favour by getting aspiring actor Rydell a part in *Wanted: Dead Or Alive*).

McQueen Quotables: Boon Hogganbeck: "Sometimes you have to say goodbye to the things you know and hello to the things you don't!"

McQueen's Cash: His, by now, standard $700,000.

The Verdict: McQueen and Mark Rydell don't come out of *The Reivers* with too much credit, but they don't come out of it anywhere near as badly as William Faulkner. While he may have won the Pulitzer Prize for the novel, it was by no means the great author's best work. For a taste of Faulkner at his finest, get hold of *Sanctuary*, *The Hamlet*, *The Sound And The Fury* or his impenetrable but intense screenplay for Howard Hawks' *The Big Sleep*. Film 2/5, McQueen 2/5.

Le Mans (1971)

Cast: Steve McQueen (Michael Delaney), Siegfried Rauch (Erich Stahler), Elga Anderson (Lisa Belgetti), Ronald Leigh Hunt (David Townsend), Fred Haltiner (Johann Ritter), Luc Merenda (Claude Aurac), Christopher Waite (Larry Aurac), Louise Edlind (Mrs Anna Ritter), Angelo Infanti (Lugo Abratte), Jean Claude-Bercq (Paul-Jacques Dion), Michele Scalera (Vito Scaliso), Gino Cassani (Loretto Fuseli), Alfred Bell (Tommy Hopkins), Carlo Cecchi (Paolo Scadenza), Richard Rudiger (Bruno Frohm), Hal Hamilton (Chris Barnett), Jonathan Williams (Jonathan Burton), Peter Parten (Peter Wiese), Conrad Pringle (Tony Elkins), Erich Glavitza (Josef Hauser), Peter Huber (Max Kummel)

Crew: Director Lee H Katzin, Writer Harry Kleiner, Producer Jack N Reddish, Executive Producer Robert Relyea, Associate Producer Alan Levine, Music Michel Legrand, Cinematographers Robert B Hauser & René Guissart Jnr, Editors Don Ernst & John Woodcock & Ghislaine Des Jonquères, Visual Designer Nikita Knatz, Production Designer Phil Abramson, Costume Designer Ray Summers, 106 minutes

Also Known As: The 24 Hours Of Le Mans, Day Of The Champion

Story: Le Mans, the greatest motor race in the world, and driver Michael Delaney is involved in an accident in which his arch-rival Belgetti dies. A year later, Delaney returns to the track. Injured again, he has his superficial wound dressed and returns to the pits where he is stopped by Belgetti's wife. Asked why he feels the need to race, Delaney delivers a moving paean to the drivers' love of speed and the need for the individual to challenge himself. With his guilt eased, all that stands between Delaney and the title are his new nemesis Erich Stahler and two dozen of the best drivers in the world. Delaney and Stahler get so caught up in their own personal battle that another driver pips them to the line. As the new champion is crowned, Delaney comes to terms with defeat.

McQueen Off-Screen: *Le Mans* was a sad film for Steve as it spelt the demise of both his production company Solar and his friendship with director John Sturges. As long ago as 1965, McQueen, Sturges and director John Frankenheimer (*Seconds*, *The Manchurian Candidate*) had talked about adapting Robert Daley's *The Cruel Sport*. When Frankenheimer left the project to make the similarly themed *Grand Prix* with Steve's fellow *Great Escape* artist James Garner, Sturges and McQueen turned their attention to making a movie about the Le Mans 24 Hour Endurance Race. Steve convinced Cinema Center to distribute the film (although they insisted it be a movie rather than McQueen's planned docudrama) but he couldn't convince Sturges about what shape the movie could take and so the director left the project. They would never work together again.

Since the film wasn't a documentary, McQueen wasn't allowed to compete in the race. Instead, he and director Lee H Katzin shot footage from the 1969 and 1970 events and then performed a mock-up of the race in the late Summer and Autumn of 1970. Unable to raise the $6 million needed to complete the movie, Solar Pictures became a holding company.

Things were no less problematic on the track. British driver Derek Bell suffered burns to his hands and face, Porsche driver David Piper lost his right leg and McQueen almost bought it in his infamous coke-fuelled crash and in a near miss with a production lorry. Asked to account for his love of racing, Steve replied, "people say that all racers are beckoning death, but it's not that way. I don't enjoy sheer speed over which you have no control. That frightens me. The challenge of racing is knowledge that your equipment is best, that you are in command. The racers I know aren't in it for the money. They race because it's something that's inside them. They're not courting death. They're courting being alive."

McQueen On-Screen: Like *The Thomas Crown Affair*, McQueen doesn't so much act in *Le Mans* as appear. Since he really is playing himself, it's no surprise, given the shoot's headaches, that he comes across as a dark, driven man - wholly unattractive but understandably sullen. While Steve's on-screen personality is unfamiliar, *Le Mans* opens with a McQueen trademark, a close-up shot of the back of his head.

McQueen's Confederates: Rather appropriately for a film shot overseas, McQueen was surrounded by unfamiliar faces on the set of *Le Mans*. The only close friends of Steve's involved in the project were his Solar associates Robert E Relyea and Jack Reddish.

McQueen's Cash: Originally promised $750,000 and gross participation, Steve waived the lot in order to retain creative control.

The Verdict: *Le Mans* must have looked pretty fancy in 1971, what with all its zooms and POV shots. Now, however, it is decidedly dated and, like most labours of love, deathly dull for all except those who were in love with it. In short, you wouldn't think 24 hours could seem such a long time. Film 2/5, McQueen 2/5.

Silver Dream McQueen

"An actor is a puppet, manipulated by a dozen other people. Auto racing has dignity. But you need the same absolute concentration. You have to reach inside yourself and bring forth a lot of broken glass."

Steve McQueen's devotion to speed was legendary. During his life, he assembled a collection of 5 airplanes, 57 cars and 210 motorcycles.

So, was he any good? Well, in 1970, McQueen participated in Florida's famous Sebring International Twelve Hour Endurance Race with a broken foot. His Porsche 908 Spyder finished first in its class and was only narrowly pipped to the overall title by race legend Mario Andretti. The future Grand Prix World Champion later commented that: "This is the closest race I've run and I'm lucky to have taken it." A delighted McQueen responded: "We never expected to do anything against all those bigger machines. We were just trying for a class win, not the overall. This is fantastic!"

Andretti wasn't the only person impressed with Steve's driving abilities. Porsche mechanic Haig Alltounian said, "I honestly believe that had Steve pursued a career in racing rather than show business, he probably could have made a living." Lotus team manager Andy Ferguson concurred ("The drivers rate Steve very highly") as did driver Masten Gregory ("I had an opportunity to do some dicing with Steve and he was driving bloody well. He's a competitor and that's very important").

He was pretty handy on a motorbike, too. Having used money from bike competitions to put himself through acting school, Steve competed for the national trials team, finished tenth out of 500 in the 1970 Lake Elsinore Grand Prix (the event in which he broke his foot) and eleventh out of 2,000 in the gruelling Desert Classic. Steve's riding exploits were catalogued in Bruce Brown's 1971 documentary *On Any Sunday*. Classified by some as an official McQueen movie, it really isn't anything of the sort - it's a film about Steve, he doesn't *star* in it. For the same reason, neither Nikita Knatz' *Le Mans And The Man McQueen* nor Steve's environmental documentary *The Coming Of The Roads* are discussed in this book.

For Steve's next film, however, he would have to get aquainted with a more old fashioned mode of locomotion...

Junior Bonner (1971)

Cast: Steve McQueen (Junior Bonner), Robert Preston (Ace Bonner), Ida Lupino (Elvira Bonner), Joe Don Baker (Curly Bonner), Barbara Leigh (Charmagne), Mary Murphy (Ruth Bonner), Don 'Red' Barry (Homer Rutledge), Sandra Deel (Nurse Arlis), Rita Garrison (Flashie), Charles D Gray (Burt), Ben Johnson (Buck Roan), Bill McKinney (Red Terwiliger), Matthew Peckinpah (Tim Bonner), Sundown Spencer (Nick Bonner), Dub Taylor (Del), Rod Hart (Singer)
Crew: Director Sam Peckinpah, Writer Jeb Rosebrook, Producer Joe Wizan, Music Jerry Fielding, Cinematographer Lucien Ballard, Editor Robert L Wolfe, Costume Designer Eddie Armand, Technical Advisor Casey Tibbs, 103 minutes

Story: Professional cowboy Junior Bonner returns to his home town of Prescott, Arizona, to visit his family and participate in the annual Frontier Day rodeo. Arriving at the Bonner ranch house just in time to see it being torn apart by bulldozers, Junior learns from his mother, Elvira, that his father, Ace, sold the land to his younger brother Curly for a knock-down price. Curly is now redeveloping the land for residential purposes. Ace, on the other hand, is laid up in hospital, where Junior finds him asleep. That evening, the Bonners descend on Elvira's for dinner. Curly and his wife, Ruth, talk endlessly about their new housing development. They want Junior to work for them as a salesman but he refuses. When Curly tells him that he should grow up and start thinking about his future, Junior knocks his brother clean out. The next day, Junior again visits the hospital only to find that his father has discharged himself. He returns to the rodeo site where he is offered a job working for livestock owner Buck Roan, but Junior turns it down. He then catches up with his father at the Frontier Day parade and learns of Ace's plan to become a gold prospector in Australia. Father and son then participates in the rodeo's wild milk race. That evening, the Bonner clan meet up in a local saloon and Curly and Junior spar for a second time. At the end of the evening, Junior takes up with a girl called Charmagne and Ace goes home with the estranged Mrs Bonner! Later on, the Bonner men return to the bar where Curly and Junior make their peace and Ace drops a bunch at the card table. Independence Day arrives and with it comes the highlight of the rodeo, the bull riding. Determined to win so that he can stay out on the road, Junior rides his arch-nemesis Sunshine for the full eight seconds and scoops the purse. He celebrates with Charmagne before heading over to the Prescott travel agency to buy a one-way ticket to Sydney for his father. He then stops by his mother's, before heading out once more onto the open road...

McQueen Off-Screen: 1971 had been a big year for Steve McQueen. He'd formed First Artists with Barbra Streisand, Sidney Poitier, Dustin Hoffman and Paul Newman, realised his ambition of shooting a motor-racing movie and got divorced from Neile, his wife of fourteen years. Steve had expected the divorce to be painful (he was hit in the pocket for over $6 million in alimony and child support, and lost access to Terri and Chad), but he hadn't anticipated the headaches that either *Le Mans* or First Artists would cause. Although it took its inspiration from United Artists (the company founded in 1919 by Charlie Chaplin, Mary Pickford, Douglas Fairbanks Snr and D W Griffith), First Artists was really an elaborate tax dodge. Disappointed with the films the company was churning out (*Buck & The Preacher* (1971, dir Sidney Poitier), *Pocket Money* (1972, dir Stuart Rosenberg), *Up The Sandbox* (1972, dir Irwin Kershner)), Steve looked elsewhere for something to do. Impressed with *The Wild Bunch*, he signed on to make *Junior Bonner* with Sam Peckinpah who Steve hadn't seen since the director was fired from *The Cincinnati Kid*.

McQueen On-Screen: To find out what I think of McQueen's performance in *Junior Bonner*, skip ahead to the chapter Sam & Steve. As for how he looks, the picture features a close-up of Steve drinking a beer that's the best advert Miller ever had. Tanned, well-conditioned and in full Western togs: McQueen never looked more beautiful on film.

McQueen's Confederates: For the next two films, Steve was to be an honorary member of Sam Peckinpah's stock company, members of which included actors Ben Johnson and Dub Taylor (who Steve had been a fan of since he'd worked with him on *The Cincinnati Kid*), editor Robert Wolfe and cinematographer Lucien Ballard.

McQueen Quotables: i) Junior: "Maybe I oughta take up another line of work." ii) Junior: "Tell 'em Junior sent ya."

McQueen's Cash: $500,000. Steve was, in fact, the one person who came out of *Junior Bonner* in profit. Grossing just $2 million worldwide, it is the only movie of McQueen's that actually lost money.

The Verdict: Of all the cinematic arts, editing is both the most complicated and the least understood. Thanks to TV commercials and MTV, people think the secret of editing is jarring, attention-grabbing cuts. However, the really great editor doesn't draw attention to his work. To find out what film editing is *really* about, take a look at the seamless job Robert Wolfe does in *Junior Bonner*. And while you're about it, take a good look at the work of Steve

McQueen and Sam Peckinpah as you won't find finer acting and directing in motion pictures, either. Film 5/5, McQueen 5/5.

The Getaway (1972)

Cast: Steve McQueen (Doc McCoy), Ali MacGraw (Carol McCoy), Ben Johnson (Jack Benyon), Sally Struthers (Fran Clinton), Al Lettieri (Rudy Butler), Slim Pickens (Cowboy), Richard Bright (Thief), Jack Dodson (Harold Clinton), Dub Taylor (Laughlin), Bo Hopkins (Frank Jackson), Roy Jenson (Cully), John Bryson (The Accountant), Bill Hart (Swain), Tom Runyon (Hayhoe), Whitney Jones (The Soldier), Raymond King (Boy On The Train), Ivan Thomas (Boy On The Train), C W White (Boy's Mother), Brenda W King (Boy's Mother), W Dee Kutach (Parole Board Chairman), Brick Lowry (Parole Board Commissioner), Martin Colley (McCoy's Lawyer), O S Savage (Field Captain), Dick Crockett (Bank Guard), A L Camp (Hardware Shop Owner), Bob Veal (TV Shop Proprietor), Bruce Bissonette (Sporting Goods Salesman), Maggie Gonzalez (Carhop), Jim Kannon (Cannon), Doug Dudley (Max), Stacy Newton (Stacy), Tommy Bush (Cowboy's Helper)

Crew: Director Sam Peckinpah, Writer Walter Hill, Novel Jim Thompson, Producers Mitchell Brower & David Foster, Associate Producer Gordon T Dawson, Music Quincy Jones, Cinematographer Lucien Ballard, Editors Robert L Wolfe & Roger Spottiswoode (consultant), Art Directors Angelo P Graham & Ted Haworth, Set Decorator George R Nelson, Costume Designer Ray Summers, Production Manager Donald Guest, Assistant Directors Newt Arnold & Gordon T Dawson & Ron Wright, 122 minutes

Story: After five years inside, bank robber Doc McCoy begs his wife and partner in crime Carol to cut a deal with corrupt politician Jack Benyon to secure his release. Benyon agrees on the condition that McCoy teams up with a couple of Benyon's goons for another bank job. One of the henchmen, Butler, sabotages the robbery and pulls a gun on Doc, only for the arch-criminal to shoot him down. As Carol and Doc flee, Butler, who has been wearing a bulletproof vest, clambers to his feet and gives chase. Arriving at Benyon's ranch, the politico tells Doc that Carol exchanged sexual favours to gain his release. Mrs McCoy shoots Benyon only to then receive a savage beating from Doc. Meanwhile, the injured Butler takes local doctor Harold Clinton hostage, together with his wife Fran, and demands that he be driven to the McCoys' ultimate destination, El Paso. The McCoys hightail it to the railway station to catch the El Paso train, but their travel plans are scotched when a thief relieves Carol of the cash. Although Doc retrieves the money, he suggests that it might be a good idea if the husband-and-wife team split up. With the thief having identified them to the police, Doc and Carol make a dash across the state. During their adventures, Doc realises just what his wife is willing to go through to be with him and he suggests a reconciliation. Arriving in El Paso, the McCoys think they're home free. But Butler and Benyon's other goons have arrived before them. A vicious gunfight ensues, during which Doc slays all the henchmen. On the lamb once again, Doc and Carol hold up a cowboy and demand that he drive them across the border. Since they like the good ol' boy, they buy the truck from him for $30,000 and then drive off into the sunset.

McQueen Off-Screen: When Steve became involved in *The Getaway*, the film was being produced by Paramount, Peter Bogdanovich was in the director's chair and his co-star looked set to be Angie Dickinson. Then Paramount dropped the picture, Bogdanovich went and shot *What's Up, Doc?* and Dickinson became unavailable. Convinced the picture could be a huge hit, Steve sought to make *The Getaway* under the auspices of the revived Solar and First Artists. When it came to finding a director, McQueen didn't hesitate in calling Sam Peckinpah (who, coincidentally, had approached Jim Thompson about a big-screen version of *The Getaway* back in the 50s). As for a leading lady, Steve approached *Love Story*'s Ali MacGraw.

There are two stories about how Steve McQueen hooked up with Ali MacGraw. The first has it that Steve seduced Mrs Robert Evans within a day of meeting her. The second says that it wasn't until the second month of shooting that Ali would so much as talk to Steve socially. Whichever tale you believe, by the time the film wrapped, Ali was all ready to tell her producer husband that she was going to divorce him and marry McQueen. Incensed, Evans flew MacGraw to a desert health spa so she could think things through by herself. As Ali's plane took off, she was tapped on the shoulder. There, sitting behind her was a smiling Steve McQueen.

McQueen On-Screen: As Doc McCoy, Steve employs his full range of acting tricks (the smile, the shirt off (within the first ten minutes), the 'over-the-shoulders' shot (here used to create a sense of foreboding before he beats up Carol)) and explores such favourite themes as the way a man reacts when the world's against him. If *The Getaway* is something of a one-note movie (director Peckinpah openly admitted that the film didn't have a second act),

Steve's is anything but a one-dimensional turn. From his crack-up at the beginning to his realisation of how much Doc and Carol need one another, Steve delivers something you rarely find in formula films, a genuinely layered performance.

McQueen's Confederates: Writer Walter Hill (now famous as the director of such manly action movies as *Southern Comfort*, *48 Hours* and *The Long Riders*) had previously worked as an assistant director on *The Thomas Crown Affair* and *Bullitt*. The rest of the cast and crew were mainly members of Sam Peckinpah's screen family: Ben Johnson, Dub Taylor, Slim Pickens, Richard Bright, Bo Hopkins, Lucien Ballard, Newt Arnold, Gordon Dawson, Roger Spottiswoode and Robert Wolfe. *The Getaway* originally featured a score by Sam's composer of choice Jerry Fielding, but Steve ditched it in favour of a theme written by Quincy Jones.

McQueen's Cash: $300,000 plus points (First Artists' charter stated that no star would be paid more than $300,000 and no film would be budgeted at over $3 million).

Legacy: *The Getaway* was remade in 1994 by Australian director Roger Donaldson. James Woods, Michael Madsen and Kim Bassinger played the parts of Benyon, Butler and Carol and fared pretty well. However, as Doc McCoy, Alec Baldwin couldn't even fill one of McQueen's boots.

If, by the way, you enjoy Peckinpah's take on the picture and you want to read Jim Thompson's source novel, be warned - it's very grim and the ending is anything but happy.

The Verdict: From the virtuoso opening sequence in which McCoy's mental disintegration is compressed into a few minutes to the blood-soaked motel shoot-out, *The Getaway* is as entertaining as it's possible for a movie to be. And McQueen's Doc McCoy is as good as bad guys get. Film 4/5, McQueen 5/5.

Sam & Steve

There have been loads of great actor/director partnerships: John Wayne and Howard Hawks, Kevin Costner and Ron Shelton, Steve Buscemi and The Coens, Kurt Russell and John Carpenter, er...

Chevy Chase and Michael Ritchie. The list could go on for pages. What makes Steve McQueen so unusual is that he formed profitable relationships with five different directors. He made two movies with Robert Wise who directed Steve to his sole Oscar nomination, shot three films with John Sturges who made him a household name, worked on two occasions with Robert Mulligan who transformed him into a romantic lead, and teamed up twice with Norman Jewison to make movies which reinforced his image as the 'King Of Cool.' While these collaborations helped make McQueen famous, Steve was to enjoy his greatest artistic success with Sam Peckinpah.

The handsome, million-dollar-a-movie leading man given to playing glib good guys and the grizzled director famed for his ballets of blood and brooding tales of Western anti-heroes - you'd be forgiven for thinking McQueen and Peckinpah couldn't have had a thing in common. While they superficially made strange bedfellows, Sam and Steve were actually cut from very similar cloth. Both ex-Marines, they'd each had difficult upbringings (Steve's turbulent, Sam's awkward), they'd both been given breaks by Don Siegel (Peckinpah as his gofer on *Invasion Of The Bodysnatchers*, McQueen courtesy of *Hell Is For Heroes*) and they shared the same love of women, liquor and the American West. They'd also both surrounded themselves with stock companies, a symbol of their belief in the positive effects of male camaraderie (Ben Johnson, Slim Pickens, Paul Fix and Dub Taylor were, in fact, members of both men's posses).

There was, though, another reason why Sam and Steve were born to make pictures together. Critics have often compared Peckinpah to America's greatest authors. Some have seen him as the cinematic equivalent of Herman Melville or Ernest Hemingway. Others have spied similarities between his work and the novels of William Faulkner. With his belief that man was a contradictory beast - majestic one moment, malevolent the next - Peckinpah was actually closer in spirit to misanthropic, sci-fi maestro Kurt Vonnegut (*Slaughterhouse 5*, *Breakfast Of Champions*, *The Sirens Of Titan*). And as Sam's movies were infused with Vonnegut-esque attitudes, so Steve McQueen was the walking embodiment of man's dichotomous nature - repulsive for his sexism, admirable for his courage.

Besides having so much in common, McQueen and Peckinpah possessed qualities that the other lacked but sorely wanted. To Peckinpah, who worked principally with character actors like Warren Oates, Ben Johnson and L Q Jones, McQueen represented stardom, exposure and big box office. For Steve, who longed to do something substantial, Sam meant class, art and an opportunity, at last, to be taken seriously.

The first fruit of this collaboration, 1971's *Junior Bonner*, isn't just one of the best movies on either man's filmography; it's one of the finest movies ever made. While Sam's contribution to the picture has been fully celebrated (the BFI's Western expert Tom Milne considers *Junior Bonner* Peckinpah's finest picture), frustratingly little has been said about McQueen's incredible performance. If you read a summary of *Junior Bonner* (to wit: *Halliwell's Film Guide* - "An ageing rodeo star returns to his home town and finds his family in trouble"), you'd assume that the title role was one that any half-decent actor could have carried off. For the tragedy of Jeb Rosebrook's screenplay to be fully realised, the lead couldn't have been played by, say, Ben Johnson or William McKinney (both excellent in their supporting roles, incidentally). Although Junior's sun is setting, he is still a somebody on the rodeo circuit. If a somebody is played by a nobody, no audience in the world is going to give a damn about his predicament. No, for Bonner's situation to have any sting, the part had to be played by a star. That the role was played by Steve McQueen, simply multiplied the pathos by the power of ten.

It isn't just Steve's willingness to use his fame to up the film's melancholy that impresses. Given the situation of his character, there must have been a huge temptation to play Junior overtly down. By employing subtle gestures instead of frowns and considered pauses instead of grimaces, McQueen makes Junior sadder than he'd have been had Steve played him forever on the brink of breaking down. Were Bonner moping about all the time, we might pity him but we wouldn't feel for him. By playing him as an upbeat guy in a situation from which the only way is down, McQueen makes us feel for him in spades.

And while we're in the business of praising Steve's work on *Junior Bonner*, McQueen also deserves a big hand for turning down the producers' idea of having Gene Hackman play Curly. Steve's reluctance to give the part to the Oscar-winning actor was probably fuelled by ego. However, the film simply wouldn't have worked had the brothers Bonner both been played by big stars. With a virtual unknown playing the successful businessman and a living legend taking the role of the fading star with an uncertain future, *Junior Bonner*'s air of tragedy reaches levels that could never have been approached had Hackman been on board.

After such an unqualified artistic success, it's a little disappointing that, when Peckinpah and McQueen paired up for a second time, they didn't attempt something equally daring. This extraordinarily entertaining picture also allowed McQueen to show a darkness and vulnerability that he'd never before shown on screen. A wife-beating coward, unable to hack his time inside and uncertain of his own capabilities, this isn't the same Steve who had us all convinced he'd clear that fence in *The Great Escape*.

It's been said that McQueen is too iconic a figure to be considered part of Peckinpah's posse. True as this might be, it's really the fact that Steve only made two movies with Sam that explains why we don't immediately associate the 'King Of Cool' with the man they called 'The Monster.' After *The Getaway*, Sam and Steve's careers went in markedly different directions. Steve made *Papillon* and *The Towering Inferno* and became richer and more famous than ever. Sam, meanwhile, gradually disappeared into a fog of cocaine and crap movies. There was a brief moment when it looked like the two might re-team for the Salkind Brothers *Superman*, but Steve had grown too fat and Sam was more interested in making a film about a *Cross Of Iron* than a 'man of steel.' While the successes of *Junior Bonner* and *The Getaway* leave us wondering what might have happened had Peckinpah and McQueen got it together again, perhaps it was for the best that they parted company in 1971.

Although they both died young (Steve in 1980 aged 50, Sam in 1985 aged 59), the duo's insatiable appetites could have sent them to even earlier graves had they hung out more. There's also no guarantee that subsequent pictures would have lived up to the high standards they'd set. After all, when Steve's *Getaway* co-star and ex-wife Ali McGraw teamed up with Peckinpah again, the end product was the execrable *Convoy.*

As Good As It Gets

After his artistic triumph with Peckinpah, McQueen returned to the business of making some good, hard cash. The salaries of his next two pictures would confirm Steve's status as the world's highest-paid film star.

Papillon (1973)

Cast: Steve McQueen (Henri Charrière aka Papillon), Dustin Hoffman (Louis Dega), Victor Jory (Indian Chief), Don Gordon (Julot), Anthony Zerbe (Leper Colony Chief), Robert Deman (Maturette), Woodrow Parfrey (Clusiot), Bill Mumy (Lariot), George Coulouris (Dr Chatal), Ratna Assan (Zoraima), William Smithers (Warden Barrot), Val Avery (Pascal), Gregory Sierra (Antonio), Mills Watson (Guard), Ron Soble (Santini), Barbara Morrison (Mother Superior), Dalton Trumbo (Commandant), Vic Tayback (Sergeant), Don Hanmer (Butterfly Trader), E J Andre (Old Con), Richard Angarola (Commandant), Jack Denbo (Classification Officer), Len Lesser (Guard), John Quade (Masked Breton), Fred Sadoff (Deputy Warden), Allen Jaffe (Turnkey), Liam Dunn (Old Trustee)

Crew: Director Franklin J Schaffner, Writers Dalton Trumbo & Lorenzo Semple Jnr, Novel Henri Charrière, Producers Franklin J Schaffner & Robert Dorfmann, Executive Producer Ted Richmond, Associate Producer Robert Laffont, Music Jerry Goldsmith, Cinematographer Fred Koenekamp, Editor Robert Swink, Production Designer Anthony Masters, Costume Designer Anthony Powell, 150 minutes

Story: Henri Charrière (known as Papillon because of the large butterfly tattoo on his chest) is a small-time crook and conman. Framed for the murder of a pimp, Charrière receives a life sentence and is packed off to French Guyana, where his insatiable desire for freedom sees him make one escape attempt after the other. While inside he befriends fellow inmate Louis Dega who helps him with his escape plans. In the end, there is nothing for the French Authorities to do but send the pair to the notorious Devil's Island, off the coast of Venezuela. Despite five years in solitary, Charrière's spirit and his friendship with Dega not only help him to survive his ordeal but allow him to mount one last bid to flee a gaol that is said to be inescapable...

McQueen Off-Screen: Set on Devil's Island but shot in Jamaica, producers Franklin J Schaffner and Robert Dorfmann declared *Papillon* a French production as a tax dodge. McQueen disapproved of such shoddy financial arrangements. When it turned out there wasn't sufficient money to pay the crew, Steve, who'd received his \$2 million plus up front, also downed tools.

To get into character, McQueen's First Artists' partner Dustin Hoffman restricted his diet to a single coconut a day. Steve, in contrast, got by on a steady diet of strong Jamaican beer and Olympic-strength skunk.

And since I've spent a lot of this book banging on about the superiority of the naturalistic McQueen over the phoney Hoffman, here's an anecdote from Marshall Terrill's *Steve McQueen: Portrait Of An American Rebel* that ought to close the book on the deal. Charles Durning, who co-starred with McQueen in *An Enemy Of The People*, was sat talking to Hoffman on the set of *Tootsie* when the subject of Steve came up. Hoffman mentioned that his *Papillon* co-star had offered him some simple acting advice. "Less, Dusty. Do less. Just throw that out, you don't need it. Keep it simple." And how did Dustin respond? "I took his advice. It turned out he was right." Yes, that's right. The two-time Academy Award-winning method man took an acting lesson from the bloke who starred in *The Blob*.

In typical McQueen style, Steve didn't perform *Papillon*'s big set-piece stunt (look closely at the end when he floats off into uncertainty and you'll see a frogman beneath Charrière's coconut mat). He and Hoffman did appear in the hairy crocodile sequence, however.

McQueen On-Screen: Although his turn in *Tom Horn* has its defenders (myself included), Steve McQueen gave his last, unquestionably great screen performance in *Papillon*. With the script giving him very little dialogue, Steve has to say everything with his body. Occasionally, he does becomes a little too wide-eyed for his own good (as in the fantasy sequences). But just check out the scene in which Papillon smokes the cigar offered to him by Anthony Zerbe's leper king and imagine trying to summon up that sort of toughness yourself. Freedom might have had more friendly faces than Henri Charrière (to wit: the chipmunk-esque Tim Robbins in *The Shawshank Redemption*) but it never had a more powerful one than Steve McQueen.

McQueen's Confederates: Old hands Don Gordon and Vic Tayback made sure Steve never ran out of reefer and Red Stripe. The cast also features Bill Mumy, aka *Lost In Space*'s Will Robinson, and George Coulouris, who played the marvellous Walter Parks Thatcher in Orson Welles' *Citizen Kane*. Screenwriter Dalton Trumbo appears as the prison camp Commandant. The beautiful bleached-out images, meanwhile, come courtesy of Steve's close friend Fred Koenekamp.

McQueen Quotables: i) Papillon: "We're something, aren't we? The only animals that shove things up their ass for survival." ii) (Papillon is contemplating a daring leap from a cliff to escape.) Dega: "You'll be killed. You know that." Papillon: "Does it matter?"

McQueen's Cash: $2.3 million which was a record for its time. Dustin Hoffman, by comparison, received only $1.25 million while director Frank Schaffner got a puny $750,000.

Legacy: Schaffner's film was spoofed in the Italian comedy *Farfallon* (1974, dir Riccardo Pazzaglia).

The Verdict: Franklin Schaffner was one of Hollywood's underrated talents. There have been loads of books on the cinema of Francis Ford Coppola, George Lucas, Steven Spielberg and Orson Welles, but look at Schaffner's filmography (*The Best Man, Planet Of The Apes*, *Patton, Nicholas And Alexandra, The Boys From Brazil*) and you wonder why nobody has ever been arsed to write about him. As for *Papillon*, it's right up there with that other great prison escape drama, the aforementioned *The Shawshank Redemption*. In fact, McQueen's terrific turn and Schaffner's refusal to overstate the film's message that hope is the very best of things (we know

Charrière escapes since the film is based on his memoirs, so we don't need to see it) give it the edge over Frank Darabont's picture, which lets itself down badly by showing Dufresne and Red's reunion. If you try to track the film down on video cassette or the revival circuit, be warned - there are cuts of *Papillon* that run twenty minutes shorter than the film's official running time. And American fans shouldn't be fooled by the PG certificate *Papillon* received in the US. The film features scenes of blood-curdling violence that small children might want to watch again and again. Film 4/5, McQueen 5/5.

The Towering Inferno (1974)

Cast: Steve McQueen (Michael O'Hallorhan), Paul Newman (Doug Roberts), Faye Dunaway (Susan Franklin), William Holden (James Duncan), Fred Astaire (Harlee Caliborne), Susan Blakley (Patty Simmons), Richard Chamberlain (Roger Simmons), Jennifer Jones (Lisolette Mueller), O J Simpson (Jernigan), Robert Vaughn (Senator Gary Parker), Robert Wagner (Dan Bigelow), Susan Flannery (Lorrie), Don Gordon (Kappy), Sheila Mathews (Paula Ramsay), Norman Burton (Will Giddings), Jack Collins (Mayor Ramsay), Felton Perry (Scott), Gregory Sierra (Carlos), Ernie F Orsatti (Mark Powers), Dabney Coleman (Deputy Chief 1), Elizabeth Rogers (Lady In Buoy), Ann Leicester (Guest), Norman Grabowski (Flaker), Ross Elliott (Deputy Chief 2), Olan Soule (Johnson), Carlena Gower (Angela Allbright), Mike Lookinland (Phillip Allbright), Carol McEvoy (Mrs Allbright), Scott Newman (Young Fireman), Paul Comi (Tim), George Wallace (Chief Officer), William Bassett (Leasing Agent), John Crawford (Callahan), Erik L Nelson (Wes), Art Ballinger (Announcer), Norman Hicks (Pilot), Thomas Karnahan (Co-pilot), Maureen McGovern (Singer, uncredited)

Crew: Directors John Guillermin & Irwin Allen, Writer Stirling Silliphant, Novels *The Tower* Richard Martin Stern & *The Glass Inferno* Thomas M Scortia & Frank M Robinson, Producer Irwin Allen, Associate Producer Sidney Marshall, Music John Williams, Cinematographers Joseph Biroc & Fred Koenekamp, Editors Harold F & Carl Kress, Production Designer William Creber, Costume Designer Paul Zastupnevich, Special Effects L B Abbott & A D Flowers & Logan Frazee, 165 minutes

Story: Architect Butch Cassidy designs a 135-storey skyscraper. But contractor Dr Kildare supplies inferior materials so it catches fire during a big gala attended by Napoleon Solo, Jonathan Hart, Pike Bishop, Bonnie out of *Bonnie And Clyde*, and Ginger Rogers' dancing partner. Fireman Virgil Hilts teams up with Butch to battle the blaze. Lots of people die, but since most of them are vain cowards like Dr Kildare, that's all right. The fire is eventually extinguished when the building's water tanks explode. Butch and Virgil then ride off into the sunset and wait around for the sequel.

McQueen Off-Screen: There has been a lot written about *The Towering Inferno*: about how Irwin Allen convinced two major studios, Warner Brothers and Twentieth Century Fox, to work on the same picture; and about how screenwriter Stirling Silliphant combined two best-selling books into one big-ass movie. All of this is considerably less interesting than the off-screen courage of Steve McQueen and the men of the Los Angeles Fire Department. Arriving back at Goldwyn Studios following lunch with fire chief Peter Lucarelli, Steve was informed that a blaze had broken out on a stage where a kids' TV show was being recorded. Without a moment's hesitation, McQueen donned his fireman's costume and set about fighting the fire. The blaze caused over $80 million worth of damage but not a single life was lost. Cynics dismissed the fire as a publicity stunt. "As if I want or need publicity," Steve replied.

McQueen On-Screen: Look under 'phoning in a performance' in the dictionary and it says 'see Steve McQueen in *The Towering Inferno*.' It's not that McQueen isn't any good, it's just that he's clearly thinking about how he's going to spend all that money (see McQueen's Cash).

McQueen's Confederates: A lot had happened to both Steve McQueen and Paul Newman since they last appeared on screen together in *Somebody Up There Likes Me*. Newman had starred in some of the biggest movies of the 1960s (*The Hustler, Hud, Cool Hand Luke, Butch Cassidy*...), but he had come to question his fame and started to dabble in the ultimate star excess, directing (*Sometimes A Great Notion, The Effects Of Radiation On Man-In-The-Moon Marigolds*). Steve, on the other hand, had just kept on getting bigger and bigger and bigger. Newman had felt threatened by McQueen before: he nixed the idea of Steve playing Sundance to his Butch. On *The Towering Inferno,* however, it was Steve who was making demands. He insisted that he receive the same fee and the same number of lines as Newman but that he be billed *above* the ageing star. Newman conceded to everything except the billing, so forcing the studio to devise a system whereby one of the stars' names would appear on the right of all the publicity material while the other would be billed slightly higher up on the left. Steve asked that he take the lower billing, shrewdly figuring that most people in the West read from left to right. With the star bullshit settled, the pair proceeded to get on famously throughout filming.

As for Steve's other co-stars, you can't help wondering whether, by this stage in his career, McQueen had it written into his contract that if he was going to be in a movie, Don Gordon was too. *The Towering Inferno* also pits McQueen opposite his old *Magnificent Seven* and *Bullitt* co-star Robert Vaughn, here once again playing a snivelling coward. Steve's *Thomas Crown Affair* love interest Faye Dunaway is also amongst the cast, but she never shares screen time with him. The film also features the broad smile and easy manner of likeable, former American football player O J Simpson. Behind the scenes, Steve's favourite cameraman Fred Koenekamp shared the cinematography duties.

McQueen Quotables: i) Building Owner: "Is it bad?" O'Hallorhan: "It's a fire. All fires are bad." ii) Roberts: "Do you think they'll pull it down?" O'Hallorhan: "They should leave it standing. A monument to all the bullshit in the world."

McQueen's Cash: Steve received $1 million up front and 15% of the gross takings. His total earnings were estimated at $14 million.

Legacy: There was talk of a *Towering Inferno II*. However, McQueen turned down Irwin Allen's $3 million fee and interest in the project quickly fizzled.

The Verdict: *The Towering Inferno*, like its sister film *The Poseidon Adventure*, might have a lot to answer for but, compared to some of today's event movies, it looks like *Citizen Kane*. As for Steve, he does everything that's asked of him but you can't escape the feeling that he is a man who can't wait to finish the movie and take a long break from Hollywood. A very long break, indeed... Film 3/5, McQueen 3/5.

Resting

It's been said that, for the four years between *The Towering Inferno* and *An Enemy Of The People*, Steve McQueen did nothing except drink beer and race his dirt bikes. In fact, Steve spent much of his 'vacation' trying to make a go of his marriage to Ali MacGraw. This he hoped to do by finding a film they could star in together. They were offered the leads in *Deajum's Wife* by Elliott Kastner but McQueen turned the project down because the execs wouldn't let him direct it. The couple also couldn't agree terms to star opposite Laurence Olivier in *The Betsy*.

Turning down pictures actually became something of a hobby for McQueen during his sabbatical. He said 'no' to *A Bridge Too Far* with close friend Richard Attenborough (too small a role), *Apocalypse Now* with Francis Ford Coppola (Steve wanted $3 million to play Kurtz, but Coppola offered him $1.5 million to play Willard) and *The Johnson County Wars* with Michael Winner ('not enough money' was the official line although it's just as possible that Steve had seen *The Cool Mikado* or *The Stone Killer* or *The Night Comers* or *Won Ton Ton: The Dog Who Saved Hollywood* or *The Sentinel* or...). And when he wasn't busy putting the mockers on his own deals, Steve was forbidding Ali from starring in Warren Beatty's remake of *Here Comes Mr Jordan*, *Heaven Can Wait*.

Steve's inability to find a vehicle left him so bored, he put his stunt skills to use in the Warren Oates movie *Dixie Dynamite*, crashing cars and motorbikes for $125 a week under the supervision of Bud Ekins. He also quit cutting his hair, stopped working out and started hitting the beer. His assault on his own image suggested that Steve wasn't only sick of Hollywood, he was sick of himself.

There's only so much time you can dedicate to self-neglect and collecting cars, however. As he told his close friends, Steve McQueen was only going to come back to Hollywood on his terms. So it was that Steve returned to the big screen in a project that was only marginally more surprising than his new look.

An Enemy Of The People (1978)

Cast: Steve McQueen (Dr Thomas Stockmann), Charles Durning (Peter Stockmann), Bibi Andersson (Catherine Stockmann), Eric Christmas (Morton Kill), Michael Cristofer (Hovstad), Richard A Dysart (Aslaksen)

Crew: Director & Producer George Schaefer, Writer Alexander Jacobs, Play *En Folkefiende* Henrik Ibsen, Translation Arthur Miller, Executive Producer Steve McQueen, Associate Producer Philip Parslow, Music Leonard Rosenman, Cinematographer Paul Lohmann, Editor Sheldon Kahn, Production Designer Eugene Lourie, Costume Designer Noel Taylor, 103 minutes

Story: In a small Scandinavian holiday town, Dr Thomas Stockmann discovers that the local spring has become polluted. He presents his findings to his brother and mayor of the town Peter Stockmann. Aware that the spring is the town's source of income, Peter decides to sit on the report. Outraged, Thomas takes the report to the local newspaper who agree to publish it, only for Peter to intervene. Upon learning of Thomas' doings, the local townsfolk band against the good doctor and his family. Thomas is left to ponder whether he should up and leave or stand and fight his brother and the system he upholds.

McQueen Off-Screen: *An Enemy Of The People* was the first of Steve's films that he had a hand in producing. Before settling on Ibsen, McQueen tried to get both Gogol's *The Inspector General* and Beckett's *Waiting For Godot* green lit. It has been suggested that Steve only made *Enemy...* to get out of his contract with First Artists. While this might have been his original intention, McQueen ended up caring about the project more than any other picture he'd embarked upon. With so many people telling him not to do it, the desire to bring Ibsen to the masses became irresistible.

McQueen On-Screen: A lot of unkind things have been said about Steve's crack at classical acting. It's as if critics forget that, during his time at The Neighbourhood Playhouse and The Actors' Studio, McQueen's diet consisted almost exclusively of Shakespeare. And while his work here isn't of Olivier-worrying standards, it certainly isn't as bad as *Neon* magazine claimed it was. And it's nowhere near as embarrassing as watching Mel Gibson prance about in his tights, acting as if the iambic pentameter was some sort of Olympic multi-event.

McQueen's Confederates: Since the film represented such a radical change in direction, it's only appropriate that none of Steve's old hands were involved in *An Enemy Of The People*. Notable amongst the supporting cast are character actor Charles Durning, who has been excellent in everything from *Dog Day Afternoon* (1975, dir Sidney Lumet) to *Tootsie* (1981, dir Sydney Pollack) and

82

The Hudsucker Proxy (1994, dir Joel Coen) and Michael Cristofer, author of the highly acclaimed play *The Shadow Box*.

McQueen Quotables: Dr Thomas Stockmann: "The masses are not always right. Were the masses right when they crucified Christ? And were the masses right when they clamped Gallileo in chains for claiming that the world was round?" (not quite "we deal in lead, friend," is it?)

McQueen's Cash: To convince First Artists to sink $2.5 million into the picture, Steve completely waived his fee (his asking price at the time was $5 million a picture).

The Verdict: *An Enemy Of The People* has been referred to as Steve McQueen's vanity project by people who obviously haven't seen the picture. Thirty pounds overweight and sporting a shaggy Charles Manson-like mane, Steve is almost unrecognisable from the handsome leading man who conquered *The Towering Inferno* four years earlier. Whatever you might have read elsewhere, the problem with *Enemy...* isn't McQueen so much as George Schaefer, a TV director with no idea of how to shoot for the big screen. Film 2/5, McQueen 3/5.

Tom Horn (1980)

Cast: Steve McQueen (Tom Horn), Linda Evans (Glendolene Kimmel), Richard Farnsworth (John Coble), Billy Green Bush (Joe Belle), Slim Pickens (Sam Creedmore), Peter Canon (Assistant Prosecutor), Elisha Cook (Stable Hand), Roy Jenson (Mendenhour), James Kline (Arlo Chance), Geoffrey Lewis (Walter Stoll), Harry Northup (Burke), Steve Oliver ('Gentleman' Jim Corbett), Bill Thurman (Ora Haley), Bert Williams (Judge), Bobby Bass (Corbett's Bodyguard), Mickey Jones (Brown's Hole Hustler), B J Ward (Cattlo Baron), Richard Brewer, Mel Novak, Tom Tarpey & Bob West (Corbett's Bodyguards), Richard Kennedy (John Cleveland), Larry Strawbridge (MacGregor), Pat Johnson (Ora Haley's Bodyguard), Jim 'Two Dogs' Burgdorf (Dart), Jerry Wills (Rash), Walter Wyatt (Isam), Bob Orrison (Matt), Fargo Graham (Auctioneer), Leo Hohler (Auction Deputy), Erik Owens (Boy At Auction), Jos Massangale, Dave Moordigian & Michael E Perry (Brown's Hole Rustlers), James H Burk & Bill Hart (Slaughterhouse Men), Dan Corry (Windmill Man), Jeffrey M Meyer (Gunfighter), Clarke Coleman (Jimmy Nolt), Mike Chambers, Bob Kern, W H Manooch & Fred O'Dell (Men In Feed Stores), Drummond Barclay (Charlie Honhouse), Chuck Hayward (Deputy Proctor), Tom Runyon (Bartender), John L Hallet & Jerry Jackson (Reporters), Larry Hollister (Bailiff), Victor Spelta (Man In Bar), Alan L Brown & Robert Elliott (Guards), Gilbert B Combs, Mike H McGaughty, Walter Scott & Rock A Walker (Horn's Capturers), J P S Brown (Padre), Lee Barton, Roe Henson & Paul Pinnt (Cowboys), Jimmy Medearis (Trick Rider), Chuck Henson & Claude Henson (Steer Riding Sequence), H P Eveetts, Jeff Ramsey, Bud Stout & Gary Combs (Horse Breaking Sequence)

Crew: Director William Wiard, Writers Thomas McGuane & Bud Shrake, Autobiography *Life Of Tom Horn - Government Scout & Interpreter*, Producer Fred Weintraub, Executive Producer Steve McQueen, Music Ernest Gold, Cinematographer John A Alonzo, Editor George Grenville, Art Director Ron Hobbs, Costume Designer Luster Bayless, 98 minutes

Also Known As: I, Tom Horn - A Last Will And Testament Of The Old West

Story: Tom Horn was one of the American West's most colourful characters. The man who tracked down renegade Apache Geronimo and arranged his surrender, Horn served with Theodore Roosevelt's Rough Riders during the Spanish-American War and worked as a detective for the Pinkerton Agency. He was also a champion rodeo rider, a prizefighter and boxing referee, a teamster with the Santa Fe Railroad, a cavalry scout, the owner of a silver mine and one of the most feared guns-for-hire in all Arizona. But rather than concentrating on the details of his extraordinary life, the picture concentrates on Horn's final three months. Hired by cattle barons to take out a band of rustlers, Horn does such a good job that he finds himself framed for murder. Since none of his employers will defend him, he is sent to hang. And as no one wants to be remembered as the man who killed Tom Horn, an elaborate gallows is built. So, not only is Tom Horn sentenced to death for a crime he did not commit, but the machinery that does him in is designed in such a way that he effectively hangs himself.

McQueen Off-Screen: It was the execs at First Artists' idea to make *Tom Horn*, not Steve McQueen's. After *An Enemy Of The People* died on its arse Steve, aware that his marriage to Ali MacGraw was at breaking point, looked for another project in which the couple could co-star. Plenty of pictures were discussed, *Nothing In Common*, *Fancy Hardware*, even *The Missouri Breaks* which was later filmed by Arthur Penn, but they all broke down as did the relationship. In November 1977, Steve McQueen filed for divorce.

Single yet again, Steve set about restarting his film career. Some big scripts had been sent to the McQueen household (*Close Encounters Of The Third Kind*, *The Gauntlet*, an adaptation of James (*Shogun*) Clavell's *Tai-Pan*), but he wasn't able to commit to any of them since his First Artists' contract was still one film from completion. Anxious to severe his ties, Steve suggested signing off with a big-screen version of Harold Pinter's *Old Friends* only to be told that, instead of tackling something so experimental, he ought to return to the genre that had made him a star in the first place: the Western. While lacing up his chaps was the last thing Steve wanted to do, it was an indignity he was prepared to suffer if it allowed him to escape First Artists' handcuffs.

Both the star and the executive producer of *Tom Horn*, McQueen also had a considerable hand in directing his penultimate movie. Don Siegel had originally been hired to helm but his artistic vision differed from Steve's and so he soon left. Elliott Silverstein (*Cat Ballou*) was then brought on board, but he walked the plank when he realised that he and Steve would never agree on anything. Then came James William Guerico, the manager of the rock band Chicago and director of cult motorcycle movie *Electra Glide In Blue*, but he was so ill-suited to the project, McQueen thought he might as well direct it himself. Since Directors' Guild laws meant an actor couldn't take over a picture once shooting had started (Guerico had shot three days worth of footage), Steve hired TV director William Wiard (*M*A*S*H, The Rockford Files*), who sat in the director's chair while McQueen and his cameraman John A Alonzo called the shots.

As for the stunt work, Steve performed everything except the final hanging sequence. "Ain't no way in God's world I'm going to get up there and put that rope around my neck," he explained to the producers.

McQueen On-Screen: "Past-it, no longer the golden boy," the words Sam Peckinpah used to describe William Holden's appearance in *The Wild Bunch* could easily be applied to McQueen in *Tom Horn*. The strain of having to lose the sixty pounds he'd put on during his self-imposed exile meant that, for the first time, Steve actually looked as old as he was, 49. McQueen was no doubt mortified to say goodbye to his boyishness, but his haggard, pained face made him perfect to play a Western legend nearing the end of the trail. His apparent indifference to the project also, perversely, aided the picture - his understatement lending his performance a fabulously melancholic air.

McQueen's Confederates: There aren't too many members of Steve's stock company amongst the cast, but there are representatives from the posses of Clint Eastwood (Geoffrey Lewis) and Sam Peckinpah (Slim Pickens, who'd appeared opposite McQueen in *The Getaway*'s excellent finale). Richard Farnsworth, who should have won the Best Actor award at Cannes for his work in *The Straight Story* (1999, dir David Lynch), had been fired by Steve in 1959 when working on *Wanted: Dead Or Alive*. As for the backroom boys, Chad McQueen worked on the picture as an assistant to the producer, who in this case was his father.

McQueen's Cash: Since *Tom Horn's* budget was cut from $10 million to $3 million during pre-production, McQueen didn't receive a penny for the picture.

The Verdict: As *Tom Horn* is a testament to Steve's acting talent, it also suggests that neither McQueen, William Wiard nor John Alonzo had any idea how to make a movie. It is a two-hour film that feels like a fortnight with performances that wouldn't look out of place in an Australian soap opera. The film is an ordeal but Steve's performance is one to treasure. Film 2/5, McQueen 4/5.

The Hunter (1980)

Cast: Steve McQueen (Ralph 'Papa' Thorson), Eli Wallach (Ritchie Blumenthal), Kathryn Harrold (Dotty), LeVar Burton (Tommy Price), Ben Johnson (Sheriff John Strong), Richard Venture (Spota), Tracey Walter (Rocco Mason), Thomas Rosales Jnr (Bernardo), Teddy Wilson (Winston Blue), Ray Bicker (Luke Branch), Bobby Bass (Matthew Branch), Karl Schueneman (Billie Joe), Mary Margaret O'Hara (Child On Subway), James Spinks (Angry Car Owner), Frank Delfino (Poker Player), Zora Margolis (Lamaze Leader), Poppy Lagos (Mrs Bernardo), Lillian Adams (Blumenthal's Secretary), Thor Nielson (Man In Blumenthal's Office), Stan Wojno (Intern), Jodi Moon (Billie Joe's Girlfriend), Kathy Cunnigham (Mother On Subway), Kelly Learman (Student), Michael D Roberts, Kevin Hagen, Frank Arno, Rick DiAngelo & Luis Avalos (Poker Players), Wynn Irwin (Informer), Ralph 'Papa' Thorson (Bartender), Mathilda Calnan (Hospital Volunteer), F William Parker (Watch Commander), Nathaniel Taylor (Trotter), Tony Burton & Morgan Roberts (Garbage Men), Frederick Sistine (Pimp), Taurean Blacque (Hustler), Alex Ross (Cliff McCurdy), Patti Clifton (Sexy Woman), Jay Scorpio (Man On Balcony), Jeff Viola (Young Patrolman), Christopher Keane (Mike), Dolores Robinson (Principal), Anthony Mannino (Policeman At School), Joella Deffenbaugh (Cashier), Marilyn Jones (Barmaid), William B Snider (Policeman), Chris Richmond (Bystander),

Willie Lee Gaffney (Card Player On Street), Debbie Miller (Car Rental Girl), Robert A Janz (Motorman), Dan Frick (Man In Car), Ramiro Medina (Low Rider), Bill Hart (Security Guard), Bill Willens (Suspect In Jail)

Crew: Director Buzz Kulik, Writers Ted Leighton & Peter Hyams, Book Christopher Keane with Ralph 'Papa' Thorson, Producer Mort Engleberg, Music Michel Legrand, Cinematographer Fred Koenekamp, Editor Robert L Wolfe, Production Designer Ronald Hobbs, Costume Designers Tommy Welsh & Denita del Signore, Technical Advisor Ralph 'Papa' Thorson, 117 minutes

Story: Bounty hunter Ralph 'Papa' Thorson is getting too old for this shit. He spends his days beating up lawbreakers and his nights rowing with his pregnant girlfriend. Dogs hate him, he can't drive and his eyesight has got so bad, he has to wear reading glasses. When it comes to bringing in bail jumpers like mean Rocco Mason, however, there really is no one quite like Thorson - a man so tough the only thing that can make him pass out is the news that he's become a proper 'papa.'

McQueen Off-Screen: *The Hunter* was perhaps the easiest shoot Steve was involved in. There was, of course, the obligatory sacking of the director - scribe Peter Hyams was replaced by Buzz Kulik. For the rest of the time, however, the set was a positively happy place. According to his colleagues, Steve was quite serene. It was almost as if he knew this was going to be his last picture and he wanted to make the experience as pleasant as possible.

It was midway through making the film that Steve gave his last ever interview. McQueen being McQueen, he didn't give such an exclusive to a leading magazine but to the *Alexander Hamilton High School Federalist*. And why did one of the world's biggest stars grant his first interview for a decade to a school newspaper? "Because I like kids."

Exactly how much Steve loved kids became apparent the day children from a rundown Chicago suburb arrived at their local sandlot to find it peppered with baseball mits and footballs. Steve paid for the athletic equipment and got Loren Janes to lay it out on the rec. As with all McQueen's charity work, this gesture didn't become public knowledge until after his death.

As for the film's fabulous 14-minute chase through Chicago, did Steve ride the roof of a speeding subway train? Did he buggery!

Not of the first time, Loren Janes copped the bumps and the bruises.

McQueen On-Screen: With his reading glasses, bathrobe, fluffy-bunny slippers and inability to drive, Ralph Thorson is certainly one of McQueen's more eccentric screen creations. These gimmicks aside, the butch bounty hunter isn't so far removed from many of the other characters Steve played. Indeed, Thorson has a lot in common with early twentieth century gunslinger Tom Horn - they each mete out justice in a rough house style and they both feel that their place in the world is threatened by the march of time. Thorson's record of having brought 5,000 people to justice also allies him with Josh Randall, the lawman that first made Steve famous. With plenty of head busting and some nice sweet set pieces (the scene in which he attends a Lamaze class is particularly memorable), *The Hunter* didn't stretch McQueen. By 1980, though, stretch was the last thing the exhausted star wanted to do. Incidentally, the real Ralph Thorson was 6' 2" and weighed over 22 stone. At 5' 6" and 150 pounds, McQueen could have fitted in 'Papa's' pocket.

McQueen's Confederates: The Hunter saw Steve re-team with his old Neighbourhood Playhouse acting buddy Eli Wallach, twenty years after they co-starred in *The Magnificent Seven. The Hunter* also features fine work from cinematographer Fred Koenekamp and the aforementioned Loren Janes, who'd doubled for Steve on *The Sand Pebbles* and *The Reivers* and helped lead the wayward Catholic boy back to the church. Steve's son Chad also worked on the picture as a production assistant. What's more, *The Hunter* features quality work from two of Sam Peckinpah's foot soldiers: editor Robert L Wolfe and, here making his third appearance in a McQueen movie, Ben Johnson. The film's inspiration, Ralph Thorson, makes a brief cameo as a bartender.

McQueen Quotables: Sheriff Strong: "Just look at us, an old sheriff and a bounty hunter, born a century too late." Ralph 'Papa' Thorson: "Nothing's changed. Just good guys and bad guys."

McQueen's Cash: Steve received $3 million and 15% percent of the gross - an extraordinary fee when you consider that the entire budget of *The Hunter* was only $8 million.

Legacy: Given both its subject matter and McQueen and director Buzz Kulik's connections with the stunt world, it's conceivable that *The Hunter* provided the inspiration for *The Fall Guy*, the dreadful 1980s TV series that starred Lee Majors (who some of you might remember from such films as *Piranha* and *Fire! Trapped On The 37th Floor*) as a stuntman who moonlights as a bounty hunter.

The Verdict: By no means his best film, *The Hunter* showed that, even after four years away from movies, Steve McQueen could still deliver a crowd pleasing performance as well as anyone. For me, the film has a lot in common with the Clint Eastwood *Dirty Harry* sequels of the 70s and 80s. Those films didn't ask a lot of their star but they did prove that Eastwood's name alone could guarantee good box office. Likewise, *The Hunter* mightn't have made huge demands of Steve McQueen but it proved that, when married with a half-decent movie, 'The King Of Cool' could still sell a lot of popcorn. A perfectly reasonable entertainment, the only disappointing thing about *The Hunter* is that it didn't provide Steve's film career with the spectacular finale it deserved. Film 3/5, McQueen 3/5.

When Heroes Go Down

"I don't believe in that phoney hero stuff."

Steve McQueen could have died in a lot of ways. A fatal bike, car or plane accident. A bout of drinking and drug taking. An unfortunate social disease. A bullet fired by a jealous lover or an insane fan. Steve McQueen could, and really should, have died in a manner that was in keeping with his extreme lifestyle. He certainly shouldn't have passed away from heart failure caused by, ironically, successful cancer surgery.

Mesothelioma is a rare form of cancer that attacks the lungs. Despite years of smoking tobacco and marijuana, it's more probable that Steve contracted his illness from a ten-day stretch in the asbestos-ridden brig of a US naval vessel or from exposure to the fire-retardant asbestos lining of the suits he wore for motor racing.

McQueen's cancer came to light soon after he finished shooting *The Hunter*. Dogged by a cough throughout filming, Steve checked into LA's Cedar-Sinai Hospital for tests. The star had already had one cancer scare in 1972 when doctors had removed a polyp from his throat. Not even the world's greatest surgeons could operate on the massive tumour that was discovered on McQueen's right lung on 22 December 1979.

Steve McQueen's brave fight against cancer consisted of a lot more than spending his last Christmas in hospital. Determined to keep the sickness out of the headlines, Steve carried on as if nothing was wrong. He attended the premiere of *Tom Horn*, he flew his airplanes, he lunched with showbiz pals like Dickie Attenborough - he continued to live the life of a big shot. In fact, McQueen made such a fine job of the charade that his illness didn't become public knowledge until a month before his death.

The end for Steve McQueen did not come in an LA mansion surrounded by lackeys and loved ones but in a small Mexican hospital in the company of strangers. When American doctors told him there was little they could do to treat his tumour, McQueen checked into a clinic in Juarez run by Dr William Donald Kelley, the creator of a revolutionary (read: highly controversial) cancer therapy. Opinion on McQueen's move to Mexico was divided. Steve's first wife Neile thought he was being exploited by a mendacious medic. His close friend James Coburn gave him his complete support (Coburn, coincidentally, would later find a remedy for his crippling arthritis in, of all places, Bury, Lancashire). Although highly unorthodox (Steve was subjected to a series of coffee enemas), Kelley's treatment was actually very successful. Indeed, it wasn't the tumours but a heart embolism, a common complication after cancer surgery, that eventually spirited Steve away.

McQueen used the months leading up to his death to set a few records straight. People he had wronged, he made up with. He even apologised to his wife for his adultery, although, McQueen being

McQueen, he couldn't simply confess. "Baby," he whispered, "I'm sorry I couldn't keep my pecker in my pants." Such a confession might not sound like too big a deal, but if you have a big ego (and Steve McQueen's was the size of Venus) apologising to those you've quarrelled with or betrayed must have been as hard as it comes.

In his twilight days, however, Steve McQueen found the power to do all sorts of things that you'd have thought beyond a mucho macho movie star. The man who had once said that God would only be number one "as long as I'm number one" went and converted to Christianity. More impressive still, McQueen discovered the courage to admit to being afraid. If you read the papers, you'll find that the word 'brave' crops up in pieces on celebrity cancer cases the way the word 'lardy' is used in articles about Marlon Brando. In openly confessing that his going to Mexico was the last ditch effort of a desperate man, Steve McQueen, a guy who had dedicated his life to poker faces and macho posturing, proved that sometimes the man who admits to being a coward is the bravest person of all.

Steve McQueen died at 3:45 on the morning of 7 November 1980. Cremated two days later, his ashes were scattered over the Pacific Ocean, 40 miles west of Hollywood.

"If I hadn't made it as an actor, I might have wound up a hood."

Reference Materials
Books On McQueen

Incredibly, there are only three books on Steve McQueen currently in print (not including this one). They are:

Steve McQueen: Portrait Of An American Rebel by Marshall Terrill, Plexus, US, 1995, Paperback, 478 pages, £12.99, ISBN 0859652319 Certainly the biggest book on Steve still available. Terrill's actually not much of a writer but he understands McQueen's paradoxical nature and he has spoken to all the right people. Recommended if only because there's so little halfway decent literature on Steve. Halfway decent is, alas, all this is.

A French Kiss With Death - Steve McQueen & The Making Of Le Mans by Michael Keyser & Jonathan Williams, Brooklands Books, US, 1993, Hardback, 200 pages, £39.95, ISBN 0837692434 Everything you could possibly need to know about a film which, while not his best, was one of the closest to Steve McQueen's heart. Pretty pricey, mind!

Steve McQueen by Jon Thompson, Portikus, US, 1998, £10.95, Paperback, 32 pages, ISBN 3928071300 Nice pictures but not a lot else.

The following are out of print but you might still be able to find copies in second-hand bookstores and remainder shops.

The Films Of Steve McQueen by Joanna Campbell

McQueen by William F Nolan A great book which is sadly no longer on the market. Worth scouring OXFAM shops for.

The Complete Films Of Steve McQueen by Casey St Charnez Not the most well-written of books, but hard to beat in terms of photos or information.

McQueen: The Untold Story Of A Bad Boy In Hollywood by Peninia Spiegel Crap, but then you probably gathered that from the title.

My Husband: My Friend by Neile McQueen Toffel 'Steve McQueen by the woman who knew him best' screamed the blurb, but this is no cheap expose by a scorned ex-wife. Instead, it's a touching account of an exceptionally good woman's attempts to understand an incredibly complex man. It says a lot for McQueen Toffel's writing and warmth that, although she openly discusses Steve's psychopathic rages and gross hypocrisy, her husband still comes out of the book as a man worth admiring.

Steve McQueen: The Final Chapter by Grady Ragsdale Unfortunately, to reach the final chapter, you have to get through a dozen equally shit ones first.

Steve McQueen: Star On Wheels by William F Nolan Not as good as Nolan's straight biography of Steve, but if you're more interested in McQueen the motorist than McQueen the movie star, this is an equally essential purchase.

Steve McQueen: The Unauthorised Biography by Malachy McCoy Like virtually all 'unauthorised' biographies, this is best handled at a distance with tongs.

McQueen On Video

The following are either currently available in the UK or have recently been deleted, which means that you might still be able to find copies in larger video stores or bargain bins.

Never Love A Stranger (1958), 0557923

The Blob (1958), 6345723, deleted

The Magnificent Seven (1960), S051268

The War Lover (1962), CC7028, deleted

The Great Escape (1963), S099232, also in widescreen S052163

The Cincinnati Kid (1965), S050135

Nevada Smith (1965), 6319383, deleted

The Sand Pebbles (1966), 1029W, widescreen only

The Thomas Crown Affair (1968), S058607

Bullitt (1968), S001029

Junior Bonner (1971), SONE7425, deleted

The Getaway (1972), S011122, also available in widescreen S015939

Papillon (1973), CC7271, deleted, available as part of a triple pack with Frank Darabont's *The Shawshank Redemption* (hooray!) and Alan Parker's *Midnight Express* (boo!) CC7886

The Towering Inferno (1974), S011253, also widescreen S015340

Tom Horn (1980), S001042

The Hunter (1980), 6305883, deleted

McQueen Documentaries On Video

On Any Sunday (1971), DM1102, see Silver Dream McQueen

Steve McQueen: The King Of Cool (1998), 3984250893, Robert Katz's excellent documentary features contributions from Steve's family (son Chad, first wife Neile, second wife Ali MacGraw), best friends (Hillard Elkins, Robert Relyea), collaborators (Robert Wagner, Peter Yates, Norman Jewison) and fans (Michael Madsen). The top-notch narration comes courtesy of Kevin Spacey.

McQueen On DVD

The Great Escape (1963), D056680

The Thomas Crown Affair (1968), D057442

Bullitt (1968), D001029

The Getaway (1972), D011122

McQueenesque Actors

Over the years, all sorts of thesps have supped from the well of McQueen. Rather than ripping off Steve wholesale, actors have tended to crib a particular aspect of his cool. Some have simply copied his hairstyle - check out Kevin Costner in *The Bodyguard* (1992, dir Mick Jackson), a film that was actually written for Steve McQueen by Lawrence Kasdan.

Harrison Ford also sported a similar haircut to Steve's in *Presumed Innocent* (1990, dir Alan J Pakula). Ford's tonsorial tribute is appropriate given the similarities between the two actors' career paths. Just like McQueen, Ford started out in TV and Z-grade movies, got his big break playing a supporting role in a big action movie (something called *Star Wars*) and went on to become the highest paid star of his day. McQueen and Ford's acting styles also have a lot in common; they each possess limited ranges (*Regarding Henry* (1989, dir Mike Nicols) shows that Harrison Ford plays sensitive about as well as Steve played comedy), they both subscribe to the 'say as little as possible' school of acting and, when needed, they can flash killer smiles.

George Clooney has also trod a road to Hollywood that mirrors McQueen's. While Steve started out in *Alfred Hitchcock Presents...* and

The Blob, Clooney cut his teeth on *Roseanne* and the remake of *Attack Of The Killer Tomatoes*. Then, as McQueen made it big on the back of a TV show and memorable performances in ensemble movies, George got his first real taste of fame courtesy of *ER*, *Out Of Sight* (1997, dir Steven Soderbergh) and *Three Kings* (1999, dir David O Russell). The actors have also both appeared in mega-budget disaster movies (McQueen *The Towering Inferno* and Clooney *The Perfect Storm* (2000, dir Wolfgang Petersen) and *Batman & Robin* (boom boom!)). If only Gorgeous George had the same mystique as McQueen, he might become a genuine icon.

McQueen On The Web

A keen motorist, Steve has so far made frustratingly little impact on the information superhighway.

The First Steve McQueen Site On The Internet http://members.tripod.com/~stvmcqueen/ - An unimaginative title for an invaluable site. An extensive FAQ section, quotes, magazine features, a bumper bibliography. All this plus a great article on Steve's pre-fame years and a detailed piece on mesothelioma, the rare disease that McQueen so nearly licked. A rare case on the Internet of first actually being best. A tip of the hat to Mr Chris Lambos!

The Towering Inferno http://home.1.worldonline.nl/~ajvdlely.html - Story boards, script changes, useful links - hot stuff, indeed.

The Sand Pebbles http://www.execpc.com/~cgarcia/index2.html - Absolutely everything you could ever need to know about the film and the book that inspired it. If only either was good enough to deserve such royal treatment.

The Steve McQueen Tribute Page http://members.aol.com/apslug/SteveMcQueen/film.html - Slightly undernourished and rarely updated but there's some useful info on Steve's early, not much cop movies. The site is dedicated to Terri McQueen.

Roger Harris's Steve McQueen Film Poster Site http://www.soft.net.uk/harris/McQueen/ - Displays an awesome collection of McQueen movie posters (573 at the last count) and lobby cards. Sells cool t-shirts, too.

The Essential Library

Enjoyed this book? Then try some other titles in the Essential library.

New This Month: **Steve McQueen** by Richard Luck
Sam Peckinpah by Richard Luck

New Next Month: **Jane Campion** by Ellen Cheshire
Krzysztof Kieslowski by Monika Maurer

Also Available:

Film: **Woody Allen** by Martin Fitzgerald
Jackie Chan by Michelle Le Blanc & Colin Odell
The Brothers Coen by John Ashbrook & Ellen Cheshire
Film Noir by Paul Duncan
Terry Gilliam by John Ashbrook
Heroic Bloodshed edited by Martin Fitzgerald
Alfred Hitchcock by Paul Duncan
Stanley Kubrick by Paul Duncan
David Lynch by Michelle Le Blanc & Colin Odell
Brian De Palma by John Ashbrook
Vampire Films by Michelle Le Blanc & Colin Odell
Orson Welles by Martin Fitzgerald

TV: **The Slayer Files: Buffy the Vampire Slayer** by Peter Mann
Doctor Who by Mark Campbell
The Simpsons by Peter Mann

Books: **Stephen King** by Peter Mann
Noir Fiction by Paul Duncan

Available at all good bookstores at £2.99 each, or send a cheque to: **Pocket Essentials (Dept SM), 18 Coleswood Rd, Harpenden, Herts, AL5 1EQ, UK** Please make cheques payable to 'Oldcastle Books.' Add 50p postage & packing for each book in the UK and £1 elsewhere.

US customers can send $5.95 plus $1.95 postage & packing for each book to **Trafalgar Square Publishing, P.O. Box 257, Howe Hill Road, North Pomfret, Vermont 05053, USA**. tel: 802-457-1911, fax: 802-457-1913, e-mail: tsquare@sover.net

Customers worldwide can order online at **www.pocketessentials.com**, **www.amazon.com** and at all good online bookstores.